Derek Tangye (1912–1996) was the author of the much-loved books that collectively became known as The Minack Chronicles. They told the story of how he and his wife Jean left behind their cosmopolitan lifestyle in London to relocate to a clifftop daffodil farm in Cornwall. There they lived in a simple cottage surrounded by their beloved animals, which featured regularly in his books. In their later years, the Tangyes bought the fields next to their cottage, which are now preserved as the Minack Chronicles Nature Reserve.

A Drake at the Door

Derek Tangye

Constable • London

Constable & Robinson Ltd.
55–56 Russell Square
London WC1B 4HP
www.constablerobinson.com

First published in the UK by Michael Joseph Ltd., 1963

This edition published by Constable,
an imprint of Constable & Robinson Ltd., 2014

A copy of the British Library Cataloguing in
Publication Data is available from the British Library

ISBN: 978-1-47210-992-7 (paperback)
ISBN: 978-1-47211-025-1 (ebook)

Printed and bound in the UK
1 3 5 7 9 10 8 6 4 2

Illustrations

Boris, the Muscovy drake, during daffodil season at Minack

1

I heard one day that my neighbour was leaving. We had been neighbours for seven years and, in view of the manner of our coming, conflict between us was perhaps inevitable. The neighbour represented the hard-working peasant, Jeannie and I the up-country interlopers.

Minack and our six acres of land belonged to his farm, although in reality it was not his farm. In the years before the last war, farms in West Cornwall were difficult to let and landowners were thankful to dispose of them under any conditions; and the conditions were sometimes these:

A prosperous farmer would rent an unwanted farm, stock it with cows, put a man of his own choosing called a dairyman into the farmhouse, charge him rent for each cow, and then let him run the farm as he wished. My neighbour was a dairyman.

Both of us, then, paid rent to the same absentee farmer; my neighbour for twelve cows, myself for the primitive cottage and the derelict land I was allowed to have with it.

On a practical basis I had the worst of the bargain. It

was a whim that led us to Minack; an emotion that made us believe the broken-down cottage edged by a wood and looking out on Mount's Bay between Penzance and Land's End, could become our personal paradise. And after seven years I still did not possess a scrap of paper which proved our legal right to the tenancy.

The reason for this dilatoriness was fear on our part. When in the beginning we pleaded for Minack, the absentee farmer clearly did not mind whether we had it or not. We had to nudge our way into his good humour. We had to be as careful as a ship in a minefield. One false move, a word too thrusting, a suggestion too bold, and we would have been retreating from his presence without a hope of return.

This was an occasion, we both felt, when logic or the legal mind would be a hindrance. It was not the moment to bargain or be too meticulous in wrapping the deal in legal language. We wanted Minack and in order to secure it we had to appear foolish. The result was no lease, all repairs and improvements without prospect of compensation, and six acres of scrubland which most people considered unsuitable for cultivation.

And there were other snags. There was the barn, for instance, within a few yards of the cottage, which belonged to my neighbour and not to Minack. Here he used to stable his horses, collecting them in the morning and returning them in the evening; and in wet weather when no outside work could be done he would clear the muck from the floor and pile it beside the lane which led up to his farmhouse a quarter of a mile away.

We had made this lane ourselves, opening up again

an ancient one by first cutting away the brush which smothered it; for when we first came to Minack the only means of reaching the cottage and the barn was by crossing two fields, waterlogged in winter.

In the autumn my neighbour used to spend days at a time in the other half of the barn 'shooting' his potatoes for January planting in his section of the cliff; and if it were a period when we were not on speaking terms Jeannie and I found it irksome.

'Did he say anything this morning?' I would ask Jeannie if she had seen him first.

'Not a word.'

Of course, there are some who say that the Cornish resent any 'foreigner' who comes to live among them. I am Cornish myself and I do not believe that such resentment, if it exists, is confined to the Cornish alone. Most countrymen if they live far from an urban area are on guard when a stranger appears in their midst. Strangers represent the threat of change, and change is the last thing the true countryman wants. He views the city from afar and is not impressed by its standards; and when in the summer the inhabitants disgorge over the countryside, a leavening of them always confirm the countryman's worst suspicions. The Cornish for the most part heave a sigh of relief when the holiday season is over and Cornwall belongs to them again.

As for individuals, the Cornish have the same basic ingredients as everyone else, the same kindliness or meanness, good humour or jealousy. It is only in obstinacy that the Cornish excel. If a Cornishman senses that he is being driven into taking a step against his freewill nothing, not even a bulldozer, will make him budge.

So our neighbour was leaving. He was forsaking his job as a dairyman to take over a farm of his own. He had won promotion by his hard work, while we now had the chance to take over not only the barn, but also those fields and cliff meadows adjacent to our own which were essential for certain expansionist plans we had in mind. We were delighted. Here was the opportunity to put sense into our life at Minack, to regularise our position by securing a lease, to act indeed in a practical fashion. It was not, however, a question of expressing a desire, and the desire materialising without more ado. We soon discovered there were complications.

The news of my neighbour's coming departure speedily spread through the neighbourhood, and young men began tumbling over each other in efforts to gain the vacant dairymanship for themselves.

The lure, in particular, lay in the cliff meadows which were renowned for the earliness of their potatoes and daffodils. Most of these were as steep as those we had cut in our own cliff, and I did not fancy them very much myself . . . we had enough hand labour already, turning the ground in the autumn, carrying down the seed potatoes, shovelling them in, shovelling them out, carrying the harvest hundredweight after hundredweight up the cliff again. And in any case I sensed the golden days of Cornish new potatoes from the cliff were over.

4

But there were other meadows cresting my neighbour's cliff that were ideal for our needs, large enough for a small tractor, and accessible to the Land Rover when it was necessary to use it. This was reason enough why we wanted them, but there was another.

These meadows were reached by passing in front of the cottage and taking the track towards the sea which led also to Minack meadows. We had watched our neighbour for seven years using this thoroughfare and we did not want to see anyone else doing the same. Minack, in substance, was remote from any habitation, breathing peace in its solitude, and we wanted to eliminate any prospect of enduring again the grit of friction.

And there were the fields around us. Had we been able to wave a magic wand we still could not have made use of all of them; but there were four surrounding Minack which, if we possessed them, would provide the twin advantage of isolation with the practical one of giving us the elbow-room vital for development.

In particular we needed flat ground for greenhouses. We already had one small greenhouse tucked in a clearing of the wood and another, a splendid one a hundred feet long and twenty-one feet wide, stretching down in front of the cottage on land that was swamp when we arrived. We felt sure that our future security lay in such factory-like protection; the only way possible to demolish the omnipotence of the weather.

We were aware, then, that we were at a crucial moment of our life at Minack. Here we were poised between stagnation and progress, an irritant and solace; and the success or failure of the action I was about to

5

take would dominate the years to come. I had decided to be bold.

The absentee landlord had by now become a good friend of ours.

'Harry,' I said to him one day, 'how about your giving up the lease and letting me have it instead?'

I knew quite well that by making this overture I was heading for a period of bargaining. He belonged to the breed who prefer this period of bargaining to its culmination; and should it be a horse he was buying, or a motorcar or a load of hay, his ultimate pleasure lay in the skill with which he had conducted the negotiations. I, on the other hand, like to get a deal over as quickly as possible. I have not the nerve of a dealer. If I know what I want, I find no pleasure in protracting negotiations provided the sum is reasonably within the figure I have decided to pay.

Nor had I, as far as these negotiations were concerned, any cards up my sleeve. I was living again the time when I first asked Harry for Minack. I had to have it, and he knew it. I was naked. I was at his mercy.

Inevitably he began to dally; and, as if I were a fish on a hook, he set out to give me plenty of line and himself plenty of play before he landed me neatly on the bank. Out came the excuses . . . he had promised the farm to Mr X . . . it had been for so long in his family that for sentimental reasons he did not wish to give it up . . . if Mr X did not have it, he would use the fields for young cattle . . . and so on. All these proposals were told with such conviction and friendliness that I would come back to Jeannie in despair.

'He won't let us have it,' I would say to Jeannie disconsolately.

It was the mood that Harry wanted to create. He knew that, keen as I was to do a deal, he could titillate me to be still keener. I *had* to buy the lease from him, and each fruitless interview only made me more frantic; a cigarette dangling from his lips, he watched me betraying my anxiety.

Meanwhile a corner of my mind was occupied by another problem. When, and if, Harry and I came to terms I would find myself a tenant not only of Minack but also of the hundred-acre farm to which it belonged.

This was absurd. I had been consumed to such an extent by the desire for self-preservation that I had ignored the implications the success of my endeavour might entail. And anyhow, would the landlord accept me as a tenant?

The landlord was a remote person who owned large estates in Cornwall and who, as is customary, employed a land agent as a buffer between himself and his tenants. He was an enlightened landowner and he possessed a zeal to preserve the countryside, not to exploit it; in particular he felt a special trust for the wild, desolate coastline where Minack was situated. His tenants were, of course, carefully chosen and his farms well managed but, and this was the key to the situation as far as I was concerned, the Minack farm was the only one on his estates which was now leased to an absentee farmer.

I now found myself in the process of conducting two negotiations instead of one, and in both I was sure to be the financial loser. I did not care. I had the same irrational, dynamic instinct which pushes a man up a mountain, the urge for conquest without a material value, to reach a halo which rewards the individual but never the onlooker. Security at Minack meant to us a way of life we loved. How do you price such an acquisition?

I outlined the situation to the land agent who needed no persuading to appreciate the chance I was giving him. I was offering, in fact, to buy the lease of a farm, and return it without charge to the landlord. It had never happened before in the land agent's experience; and yet, fortunately, he had enough subtlety of mind to realise there was guile behind my offer.

I was expecting payment, but the payment was not to be made in pounds, shillings and pence. I was asking for the fulfilment of my plan to secure a direct lease for Minack together with the extra land I required; and I was also asking to propose my own nominee for the farm proper.

Such an arrangement would enable the landlord once again to have direct control of Minack and the farm; and we would have the peace we sought. A secure lease for ourselves, a co-operative neighbour of our own choosing.

As it happened I already knew whom I wanted to have the farm. I had stopped the Land Rover by the milk stand which corners our long lane and the main road a week or two previously when a young farm worker called Jack Cockram came up to me. He had heard the farm was vacant and could I put in a good word for him?

At the time, of course, I could be of no help. I had neither the ear of Harry nor of the land agent, and so there was nothing I could do. But I knew the occasion was important. I had always liked Jack. He had been a wartime evacuee on the farm where he was now a skilled farmworker. He had married Alice Grenfell, niece of Jim Grenfell who kept the inn at St Buryan, and they lived in a council house in the village with their one little girl and were soon to have another.

He was plainly a type who could become a good farmer and yet, because of lack of opportunity, he would be more likely to remain a farmworker for the rest of his life. Both Jeannie and I now began to experience great pleasure that not only was there the prospect of benefiting ourselves but also the possibility of launching this couple into a new life. And so, as soon as the land agent had given tacit approval to my suggestions, I determined to complete my negotiations with Harry.

I had no need to force the issue. The evening I saw him he too had decided the time of dithering was over. I thought his proposals were perfectly fair, and I promptly accepted them. He had gained from the sale of the lease the amount he would, in any case, have received in due course from the rents of myself and my neighbour. But there was one aspect of the deal from which he could claim a victory. It was indeed a handsome victory; and when I returned from the meeting to Jeannie my elation was tempered by this subsidiary problem which now faced us.

'Jeannie,' I said, 'we are now the owners of twelve useless cows.'

My concern was due to these particular cows being classified as reactors, which meant they had failed to pass the tubercular test examination. Up to a year or so before this would not have mattered as there were scores of farms in Cornwall with reactor cows. But there had now been a Government edict ordering all cows to be tested, and those which failed had to be destroyed and sold only for meat consumption. The deadline for this edict was at the end of this particular year.

The result had been that the value of such cows had nose-dived; yet I had contracted with Harry to pay him the price of eight years before, the same valuation of the twelve cows with which he had stocked Minack when my neighbour, the dairyman, was installed.

I was further hampered by my inability to set about selling the cows until Michaelmas Day when my neighbour departed. The only thing I could do was to study the cattle markets of various centres in Cornwall, and to stare at the cows themselves as they munched in the fields around us.

As they were now entities in my life, I inevitably began to feel sorry for them; but I also discovered the streak of the businessman was becoming alive in me. I was paying £35 for each of these cows and according to the markets they were not worth £15 a piece; and already the flush of my triumph in securing the lease had started to dissolve into an unhappy feeling that I was wasting a great deal of money. I waited for Michaelmas Day.

At midday the cows became ours. Twelve cows peacefully grazing in a meadow − £420 worth. They looked so content and handsome chewing the grass, the Guernsey buff against the green, the dark Minack wood behind them and in the distance the sea, that Jeannie and I found ourselves marvelling at the toughness of people who can deal in animals as merchandise. The first and last time we were ever to sell an animal. And the sooner it was done the better.

Jack Cockram, now installed at the farm, had agreed to look after them, but he too urged speed although for a different reason. The cows might get ill and then I would be worse off than ever; Thursday was market day at Penzance and the best thing I could do would be to arrange for a haulier to collect them. But I had observed that the prices at this market had been lower than anywhere else. It was Monday and I had two days to decide.

Meanwhile I had a most unexpected piece of good fortune. As the new owner I received the cow dossier, a document containing the history of each cow, and to my delight I found that one of them was not a reactor after all. It had passed the test. It was the equivalent of a thoroughbred. In a matter of seconds this particular cow had shot up in value from £15 to over £70. And there was more good fortune soon to come.

On Tuesday afternoon around four o'clock, at a moment when I was pacing the sitting room discussing with Jeannie what we should do, a car arrived; and when I looked out of the window to see who it could be, there was Harry getting out of one door and another man, in a faded tweed suit and a weather-worn trilby, getting out of another. This was the first occasion that

Harry had arrived at Minack without being the boss. I wondered why.

It was an endearing reason. Having completed the deal with me, having tasted his victory, he had an unsophisticated wish to soften the difficulties in which he knew I would be involved. He had brought me a cattle dealer. Here was a man who, if I agreed to his offer, would carry the cows away and I would never have to see them again. It was an idea which had a special appeal to Jeannie.

I found myself, then, with Harry sitting on one side of me on the sofa and the cattle dealer on the other, while Jeannie, after a hurried instruction from me, was in charge of dispensing the beginnings of a bottle of whisky.

Harry, because that had always been his intention, performed the task of breaking the ice and he did so by extolling the virtues of the cattle dealer. He was an old man, and I felt that he carried with him the sniff of cattle on the move from one place to another; and, although he belonged to a world of human beings with whom I had no common denominator, I had enough zest for opportunism to listen and not to contradict.

The price discussion began. Out of the corner of my eye I admired the polish with which Jeannie removed one empty glass, refilled it, then watched again as that too became empty. Harry meanwhile, having unloaded his charm, slipped quietly into a corner, listening but taking no part.

I found a wonderful toughness within me that I had expected to be smothered by the threat of failing to complete a deal. Why does one have to wait for an emergency to be aware of the secret self? I can cope with the emergencies of my old life, the instant quick adjustments when countering the moves of those on similar wavelengths; but I fumble when faced by those with whom, except in the matter of the moment, I have nothing in common.

So there I was discussing the price of these cows when I saw Jeannie disappear out of the front door. One does not embark upon the kind of life I was leading unless one's wife is so part of it that one never for one second has to consider her as one of its problems. Never begin if there is doubt on either side. This is an adventure which is doomed unless it is shared . . . and there was Jeannie disappearing out of the front door.

I had now become increasingly confident, a wave of unreality had taken charge of me and I was talking about cows to this cattle dealer as if I had myself been a dealer all my life. I did not believe my voice . . . 'Give me £25 each for the lot and it's a deal.'

I learned in due course that this was the moment when Jeannie felt she could do nothing more. She felt I was among wolves. Her affection was tested not by offering any practical help, but by releasing me from her presence; as if she, because of her familiarity, might bring doubt to me as to whether or not I was capable of standing up against so strange a creature as a cattle dealer.

She took a walk to the cliffs, and looked down on the sea of Mount's Bay. It is a sea which is always reassuring. It has the familiarity of the street outside other people's homes. For Jeannie, at that moment, it had the reassurance to bring her back to the cottage with the certainty that all was well.

And all *was* well. As she came up the path from the cliff, the cattle dealer was signing a cheque using the bonnet of his car as a desk . . . and the price for each reactor cow was £23.

Harry was looking for a cigarette and I gave him one.

Now we were ready for the next stage of our life at Minack.

2

Jane was with us now. She had knocked at the door of the cottage one August evening the year before while Jeannie and I were having supper. She wore jeans, sandals, and a dark-blue fisherman's jersey. Hair, like a pageboy's, fell the colour of corn to her shoulders; she was tiny, and yet there was about her a certain air of assurance, a hint of worldly confidence which belied her childlike appearance. She was fourteen years old.

'I'm Jane Wyllie,' she announced, 'I want to work for you.'

There was no sound of the soil in her voice. It was a bell, a softly pitched bell and her words came pealing out in a rush; as if they had been rehearsed, as if a pause would break the spell of childish enthusiasm with which she was flooding the cottage. Neither Jeannie nor I dared interrupt. We had to wait until her role had been played, watching blue eyes that seemed to lurk with laughter, paying proper attention to an intense performance designed to prove her services would be invaluable.

Her mother said later that a relation had declared that Jane was deadly; meaning that Jane, once she had made up her mind on the course to take, was never to be deterred. She overcame obstacles by smothering them with her tenacity. She did not, like some, leap over them in the zest of temporary emotion, landing on the other side only to find the thrill had disappeared. She crawled to her goal and, once there, blossomed her achievement by being content.

Her plot, in this particular instance, was a simple one; for Jeannie and I were to be the means by which she would be able to leave school. We were the pivot of her future. If she could win us, total strangers as we were, over to her side she would be able to defeat an array of schoolmistresses, relations and friends who were urging her to pursue a scholastic career. We were, therefore, unsuspectingly the ace up her sleeve. We sat in innocence and listened.

She was at a boarding school near Salisbury and as she would be fifteen that November she would be old enough to leave at the end of the winter term. Her headmistress looked upon the prospect with displeasure; because, it seemed, she possessed the kind of brains which could be moulded into the pursuit of a conventional career. At this point, unknowingly of course, she had struck a chord of sympathy in both Jeannie and myself. Both of us carried the memory of youthful rebellion, and neither of us had ever regretted it. Jane had begun to seep into our affection.

Her home life, we learned, had been haphazard; and when she began to tell us about it she lost her tension, bubbling a tale of the nomadic adventures of her family as if there had never been any sadness in their substance. A farm in the New Forest, another on Bodmin Moor, another at Wadebridge . . . there were so many homes that I lost count and yet the theme, as she told of them, was one of happiness despite the plain fact that the story was one of a family struggling financially to survive.

I realised as I listened that here was a girl, young as she was, who appraised the values of life by the events she experienced rather than by what she was told. She was off the main road of convention rambling in the scrubland discovering pleasures that were hidden to others; and as she talked it became clear that she had a remarkable mother.

It was the impetus of her mother's new job that had pushed her to Minack. The family, for practical reasons, had now split up. One older sister had married, another had become a groom in a riding stables, her father had entered the hotel business, and her mother had now become herdswoman at the neighbouring farm of Pentewan. She had arrived at the end of July from her previous job at Wadebridge together with Jane, Jeremy who was nine, Acid a brindle bull terrier, Eva a griffon, Sim a Siamese cat, Val a white Persian, Polly the parrot who had belonged to Jane's grandmother, and Lamb. Lamb was now a sheep.

The farmer, a quiet fellow, from whom it happened I rented two acres of cliff land, had viewed the arrival of the Wyllie gang with surprise. He had expected only the herdswoman whom he had interviewed in a Truro hotel; but the caravanserai had arrived in a van with an élan which drove him into silence.

He greeted them doubtfully at the farm, then sent them on down the cobbled lane to the cottage which was to be their home.

It was the centre one of three that were strung together, posted above a high cliff, a cliff which plunged in stages to a sea that was restless even when the wind was light. And when the storms raged, spray drifted over the cottages, windows were filmed with salt, and sometimes the gales in their fury punched open the doors, spewing like a jet inside.

Gulls swept above the rocks below, and cormorants sped over the waves, and on the inaccessible cliff to the left a colony of jackdaws spent the day long in endless chatter. At places below the cottages, wondrous to a stranger, were shadows of once cultivated meadows lodged in the cliff like crevices. Who thought they were worth creating? Jane was to find them and to this day there is one where the daffodils she planted still bloom in the spring. There was no electric light in the cottages, no indoor sanitation, and water, except for a trickle of a well, was drained from the roof. The main road, and the bus stop, were a mile away.

Each cottage had a small garden with a gate that opened on to a narrow field which broadened as it went eastwards until it met another, a huge one leaning towards the panorama of Mount's Bay like a giant carpet of green. At the distant end was a low stone wall. Over this into another field, and halfway across the tip of Minack chimney comes into view, then its

18

massive width, then the roof. So many countless times was Jane to come this way; and when the gales blew she either had to fight head down for every yard she covered or had to race across the ground like a feather in the wind.

I looked at her now as she sat neatly on the edge of a chair. She was dainty, small hands and feet, and although her figure was sturdy she did not suggest the stamina for a landgirl.

'What does your mother say?'

'Mum's not quite certain, but if I get a job . . .'

Her mother was in the quandary of all mothers. The age of breaking away, the taut arguments which swing this way and that, the rampaging emotions of love and responsibility, so anxious to act for the best, not to be selfish, not to yield to the temptation of keeping a child at home when the horizons await.

'Mum wants me to do what I feel I want to do, and I want to work on a flower farm.'

No wonder we were the ace up her sleeve. Five minutes' walk over the fields and she would be home. A job, in fact, on her doorstep. A home where her mother would be with her and her animals around her. We were her only chance. There was no other market garden in the neighbourhood who would need her; and neither did we.

'Jane,' I said gently, 'you see we don't need anyone like you. I've a man helping me and I don't want anyone else.'

She flushed, and her eyes wandered away from mine; and there was a silence except for Hubert the gull who chose this moment to cry for his dinner from the roof.

'That's Hubert,' I said, grateful for the distraction, 'he's very old and I don't think he'll be with us much longer.' Jeannie had gone outside and thrown him up a slice of home-made bread, and the silence had returned. I did not doubt that Jane would be useful but another wage, however small, only added to our expenses. And yet ... enthusiasm cannot be priced.

'Perhaps,' I said, 'when you get back next term you'll find you want to stay on after all.' And then, yielding a little, I added, 'if the winter flowers do well we *might* be able to give you a couple of days a week after Christmas.'

We did not see her again until the first of January. I had almost forgotten her. Unaware of her character I imagined her visit had been a passing whim and some other excitement was now occupying her mind. Suddenly, however, I looked out of the window at eight o'clock on New Year's Day morning, and there was Jane coming up the path to the cottage.

'Heavens,' I said to Jeannie, 'the girl's here. What on earth am I going to say?'

There was no need for me to worry. Within a fortnight she had nudged her way into our life. Within a month we had engaged her permanently.

Geoffrey was our mainstay at the time. His home was in our village of St Buryan where generations of his family had lived. He was in his early thirties, strong as an ox, and the fastest picker of daffodils I have ever seen. He raced through a bed of daffodils as if he were some special machine devised to do the work automatically. The art of such picking lies in turning your hand backwards, burying it in the foliage, then moving forward, breaking the stems off at the base until your hand can hold no more; each handful is dropped on the path and collected into the basket when the length of the bed has been completed. As always the final skill lay in instinct. Geoffrey had an uncanny knack of inevitably picking the right stem; for myself, if I tried to go too fast, I would curse myself for picking a daffodil still green in bud.

He was a good shovel man. This is an outworn phrase today but when we launched our ambitions at Minack, a man who was so described by his fellow villagers was among the labouring elite. The area was greatly dependent on cliff meadows and such meadows could not be dealt with by machine. The long Cornish shovel was the master. It turned the ground in the autumn, it planted the potatoes, it dug them out, and in August it was at work again planting the daffodil bulbs.

'He's a good shovel man,' therefore became a testimony as powerful as one given to a Rolls-Royce engine.

I have spent many hours of my life behind Geoffrey and his shovel. I felt humble as I watched him for there was a polish about his actions which I could never hope to emulate. Just as he picked daffodils with style, so did he use his long-handled shovel.

And there was Shelagh.

We first met her in the square outside St Buryan

church and we left her on that occasion without knowing her name or having any idea that she was to become for ever a part of Minack. We had A. P. Herbert staying with us at the time and one morning when we had gone up to the village a cluster of people had gathered around us, autograph books in hand, pressing A.P.H. for his signature.

Sometimes at such moments autograph hunters are like moths round a candle; they see one of their number collecting a signature, and they press forward themselves without knowing the identity of the celebrity whose signature they are seeking. Something is up, they realise, and they must not be left out.

Among this particular cluster were a number of children who, because of their age, had no real reason to know of A.P.H.'s distinction; and one of them was a young girl about twelve years old with mousey-coloured hair and pink cheeks who hovered shyly in the background, notebook in hand, until everyone else having received their autograph, she moved forward.

By this time it was perfectly clear that none of the children had the faintest idea who A.P.H. could be. He had gently asked each one, and each one had only been able to reply in a mumble. He, of course, was not upset at all by this. He only asked the question to bring life to a situation which might otherwise have been embarrassingly silent. Then up came Shelagh.

'I'll give you a shilling if you can tell me who I am,' smiled A.P.H. taking her notebook and beginning to scribble. Shelagh blushed confusedly and looked down at the ground.

'Sir Hubert . . . or something,' she blurted out.

Even then, unknowingly, she had become a part of Minack. For a gull that summer had begun to haunt our cottage, sweeping inland every day from the cliffs, perching on the roof, watching us as we went about our business, splendidly emphasising a sense of community with the wild.

'An old gull it'll be,' someone had explained to us, 'it won't be with you long. They often start coming to a habitation when their time is near.'

For that reason we had given it no name. If it were soon to die it was better for it to remain anonymous. So when it sailed to us out of the sky, one would call to the other: 'The gull's here!' Just a nameless gull out of the hundreds which passed daily over Minack. And yet, as week after week passed by, and it became as familiar to us as the chimney beside which it strutted, we began to realise that sooner or later it must have a name. The gull had character. We found ourselves accepting its company in the same natural way as the sight of Monty our cat, stretched on a wall in the sun.

It was up there on the roof that morning we returned from St Buryan. We drove up the lane in the Land Rover, pulled up outside the cottage, and as I switched off the engine, the gull suddenly put back its head, pointing its beak to the sky, and began to bellow the noise of a bird-like hyena.

'That,' said A.P.H. in mock solemnity, 'is a protest against my being called Sir Hubert . . . or something.'

From then on the gull had its name. For no other

reason than this he was known to the end of his days as Hubert. He had a long time to go; and, as I will tell, Shelagh was with us when one day years later he came to us dying, shot through the foot by an airgun.

But at the time of Hubert's christening, we of course did not know the name of the girl who had inspired it and we did not see her again for a year or more. Then her mother by adoption, who had a house in the village, came to help Jeannie in the cottage once a week, and when she was not at school Shelagh came too.

She was very shy. Some who grow up without ever knowing the love of their true parents develop a grudge against society; and who is to blame them? Unwanted from birth, they have reason to punch at life like a boxer hitting his opponent in the ring. They carry with them an unremovable scar. Their creation was a careless indulgence yet they, not their true parents, pay the penalty. I do not think it would be easy at times to be calm if one was one of them.

But there are others, and Shelagh was one, who suffer the hell of no confidence, who pursue their lives in a secret world in which kicks are expected; who, though yearning for affection, cannot believe it can be gained without hurt. They are suspicious without being cynical. They seek for ever to give and find the love their sweet natures were born to receive.

Shelagh came from St Buryan parish but spent the first few years of her life in the north country with the couple who had adopted her. When they retired they came to live at St Buryan; and inevitably everyone in the village knew of Shelagh's secret. In a village where people were not so kind this might have been a bitter experience but no one, not even the children, ever made her deliberately aware that they knew of it. Yet she must have known that she was pointed at. She certainly knew she was pitied.

She blushed easily and was very silent; and when she did say a few words she mumbled them so that they were difficult to hear. She was, however, extraordinarily intelligent. We never had to tell her twice how to carry out a task, even in those first days when she was still at school; and if we praised her she greeted it with surprise.

She was learning to be a seamstress, and was already an excellent one; and so Jeannie used to give her socks to darn, zips to put in, the hem of a skirt to be altered, curtains to make, and so on. She used to take whatever it was home with her, and when she returned she would timidly ask for some tiny charge which Jeannie used immediately to treble. Jeannie, because they were of the same size, used to give her clothes she no longer needed herself; and I remember a tweed suit which Gertrude Lawrence had given Jeannie when she was playing in *The King and I* on Broadway. Shelagh was wearing it one Saturday afternoon when I saw her gaily sauntering down Market Jew Street in Penzance. The mark of Fifth Avenue on a waif.

When her mother by adoption stopped working for us, Shelagh continued to come on Saturday or Sunday mornings. We did not specifically ask her to do so, but she would arrive and start doing something useful like cleaning the shoes or, during the flower season, washing out the jam jars and galvanised pails. And there was one occasion, the first in which she played a vital part in the pattern of our life, when her presence seemed to us to be beyond value.

Jeannie and I had developed an idea in which we believed lay our flower-farm fortune. It was one of those ideas which come to you in the middle of the night and, to your surprise and delight, appear still just as bright in the middle of the following afternoon. The idea was to exploit the urge of holiday visitors to acquire mementoes by offering them a neat pack of daffodil bulbs. Instead of the factory-made light-houses, ashtrays and other ornaments, I would offer them something that was genuinely Cornish. They would look at their daffodils the following spring and happily remember their holidays of the previous year; and as daffodil bulbs need not necessarily deteriorate, each future spring would give them the same pleasure. Something alive to take back from Cornwall, instead of a tasteless inanimate object from a gift shop.

Nor did we have any competitors. Pre-packs at the time had not yet entered the bloodstream of the public, and certainly no one had thought of pre-packed Cornish bulbs. They were to do so, of course, the following year; but Jeannie and I were the pioneers, and the pathfinders for the big growers who thought our idea such a good one.

We now had to put our plan into effect; and there was a brush between Jeannie and myself. It was January, and though the holiday season was six months away we had immediately to begin our preparations. The fundamentals were clear. We would use for the packs the bulbs of those daffodils which we had found commercially uneconomical. We would begin digging them up when the foliage had died back in the middle of May or the beginning of June; and we would distribute the bulbs in one-pound packs to any gift shop in Cornwall which would take them. My difference with Jeannie was that I wanted to begin cautiously with a plain polythene pack and a suitable label attached, while she insisted the secret of our success would lie in an attractively designed pack which caught the eye.

I compromised by agreeing to seek the advice of an expert, and in due course the gentleman arrived at the cottage. He represented a huge company. He was a merchandise expert dealing with a vast variety of pre-pack designs throughout the country. He was smoothly self-important. He crushed me with facts, figures and theories until inevitably I realised he had his noose around my neck. I had to surrender unconditionally to such a man. He *knew* how to sell a product whether nylon stockings, washed carrots or bulbs. He possessed the magic link between the idea and the tick of the cash register. We were lucky indeed to have found him.

We had, therefore, an elaborate design for our pack. It was in three colours, red, yellow and green. There was the map of Cornwall in yellow with certain holiday centres such as Newquay and Falmouth marked in black, a gay sketch of daffodils in bloom backed by a sheaf of green foliage; and in bold red letters at the bottom of the polythene bag the words, Bulbs From

Cornwall. It was very effective. And it was crowned by a splendid idea of the expert. Balancing the design in large red letters were the two words, Lamorna Pack, and underneath in tiny letters, Packed by Tangye. Thus we had skilfully imposed upon the public a trade name. Throughout the land the public would be asking for *our* pack.

For by this time, and after several visits, the imagination of the expert had taken wings. We were now close friends. I looked forward to his visits with excitement for he conjured up prospects of our future prosperity so lush that I began to wonder where the bulbs were going to come from with which to fill our packs. Our sales would not be limited to Cornwall. We would compete with the imported Dutch bulbs. We would make use of the magic name of Cornwall and sell our packs throughout the country. The potential sales were enormous. My friend knew of city stores who would queue up for our supplies. I even began to worry that the object of our escape to Minack might be defeated. Supposing we ended up by having a factory?

We now had to decide how many packs to order. Before the expert had become my friend I had been thinking in terms of a couple of thousand, but now the picture had become so rosy that I had to think in the role of an imaginative businessman. After all, as the man pointed out, his firm would not be able to replenish our supplies at a moment's notice; it would take at least six weeks and might we not lose in that time the flush of our sales? And there was another point, a very old point as far as salesmen are concerned. The more we bought, the cheaper per thousand they would be. It was a tempting situation.

We were being encouraged, meanwhile, by our friends and those with gift shops who would stock the packs. We were flattered by their applause and delightfully deceived by their enthusiasm. Ours was a gimmick that could not fail. A small fortune lay ahead of us. We would be fools not to prepare for such success with verve. We ordered twenty thousand. And it was their arrival which gave me my first apprehension.

Ours is a long lane, narrow and twisting, and the turning space in front of the cottage is confined. It is a major task for a lorry to turn. The prospect of one trying to do so is always disquieting. And on this occasion on a peaceful Friday in the first week of June when Jeannie caught sight of the lorry lumbering slowly down the lane and shouted: 'British Railways are coming!' . . . I suddenly found my confidence ebbing swiftly away from me. I had had good ideas before in my life so why should this one succeed when others had failed?

The threat from the lorry did not materialise. It turned without mishap and as it bumped away, Jeannie and I were staring at a huge cardboard packing case it had left behind. Again I had a sense of foreboding.

'£120 worth of polythene,' I murmured as I stuck a knife into the edge of the case. I tore the top off, and there were our Packs. A vast concourse of Packs, sandwiched together, thousand upon thousand of them, the map of Cornwall a shining yellow, the clarion call of

Bulbs From Cornwall a gleaming red. It was immensely impressive. My friend, true to his word, had done an expert's job.

'They're marvellous,' said Jeannie happily.

My morale had many times been boosted by Jeannie's buoyancy. She attacks a problem without burrowing too closely underneath it and thus balances my sense of realism which I so often find depressing.

'Perhaps they look marvellous,' I said lugubriously, 'but we have to fill them *and* sell them.'

It was her luck, however, that at this very moment a car arrived and out of it stepped a handsome young man who explained he had a gift shop at Land's End. He had heard, he said, that we had packed bulbs to sell and could we let him have a hundred Packs as soon as possible?

Land's End! The prospect of having an outlet in this memento paradise seemed equal to winning a football pool. I was instantly at the other end of my personal see-saw. I was more excited than Jeannie. I visualised the hordes disgorging from their coaches and cars, posing beside the Last House in Britain, and returning from whence they came with our Pack in their bags.

'We must get Shelagh tomorrow to help us,' I said urgently to Jeannie, 'this is our great chance.'

The three of us worked throughout Saturday and it was the charm of Shelagh that, young as she was, her enthusiasm was as great as ours. It was always to be thus. Some days, of course, she was to have her moods like everyone else and I would say to Jeannie:

'What's wrong with Shelagh today?' I would ask sometimes the same question about Jane. But neither, when later the two of them were the backbone of our work at Minack, ever failed to give us the enthusiasm we hoped for.

Shelagh had quick hands. In front of us on the bench of the packing shed we had cardboard boxes in which were heaped the various kinds of bulbs. Hospodar and Lucifer and Bernardino, Sunrise and Laurens Koster and Croesus. We had bought these bulbs when first we had come to Minack, because they were very cheap and we did not know the blooms were no longer wanted in the markets. To us they were beautiful to look at; but daffodils have fashions, and these to the salesmen of Covent Garden were as incongruous as the costumes of the Twenties. They consumed, however, the same time and expense in picking, bunching and sending away, as daffodils which fetched three times their price.

But now at last they were rewarding us. A few of each in every Pack, then on the scales and off, a wire clip around the neck of the Pack, and it was ready to join the others. Jeannie at one end of the bench, I in the middle, Shelagh at the other; and for every Pack that I filled, Jeannie and Shelagh filled two. It was tiring. We had to concentrate. But never throughout that Saturday did Shelagh pause. She was only fourteen.

In the late afternoon Jeannie and I set out for Land's End, the Packs grouped in boxes in the well of the Land Rover. It was a moment of high expectation; and when we joined the line of cars heading for the

31

conglomeration of buildings, higgledy-piggledy like litter, which lay lumped at the end of the road, we were blind this time to the ugliness of the crowds. Land's End, for us, had only been a place to visit in winter; when the seas were lashing the Longships, and the sun was setting angrily, and mysterious cargo boats struggled on their course, and we were alone except for the seagulls. But on this afternoon the crowds were our friends. The jammed car park was a delectable sight. The coaches, spilling out vast quantities of the human race, presented us with notions which would have even excited the manager of a Marks and Spencer's. What potential sales! Six packs per coach and this first supply would be gone in a morning. And there were still all the other holiday centres of Cornwall.

'Jeannie,' I said, as we arrived at the Gift Shop, my voice firm with conviction, '*this* is the moment we have fought for.'

I do not know, even now, what went wrong. I think perhaps our idea was ahead of its time. More likely we did not possess the flair to exploit our opportunities. The art of salemanship requires a toughness that is not part of our characters. Neither of us can bargain, and we are too easily bruised if a stranger by his manner makes us feel we are living the role of a petitioner.

That summer we roamed Cornwall with our Packs. True we covered our expenses but the prairie fire we expected never materialised; and without the urge of instant success our enthusiasm flagged. The holiday-makers preferred Midland-made hardware to our bulbs, and not even the eye-appealing, cunningly designed front of our Pack could persuade them differently. Our friend the merchandise expert had been proved wrong.

We never saw or heard of him again. He had proved himself an excellent salesman and he had left us something to remember him by. It is still there in the packing shed. A huge cardboard packing case. Nineteen thousand empty Packs inside.

Shelagh left school the following year and went to work as a domestic help on a farm. We seldom saw her. A year or so later she left to join a number of girls on a large flower farm near Penzance; and, in order to save her money on the bus fare, she used to bicycle to and fro from St Buryan, up and down the hills, undeterred however bad the weather.

One day, as she was leaving work, her bicycle skidded and she fell off, so injuring her head that she was for ten days on the danger list. It was, of course, some weeks before she was fit again to work and by this time she had lost her job. One morning she arrived white-faced at our door. She looked as if a long period of convalescence was essential.

But I knew without her speaking why she had come. Jobs are difficult to find for girls in West Cornwall and so it was inevitable that she should think of us. She had walked the three miles from St Buryan; and if during this walk she had been reciting to herself the phrases she planned to use, all she now could blurt out was: 'Have you got a job for me?'

There was no job. She was just too late.

'You see,' I explained, before driving her back to

St Buryan in the Land Rover, 'we have just taken on a young girl. Jane . . . Jane Wyllie.'

I wish I had known at that moment that these two were to become such close friends. The lost look on Shelagh's face would not have been necessary.

Shelagh, Jane and Jeannie in a
Minack daffodil meadow

3

The first task we gave Jane was looking after the sweet peas in the long greenhouse in front of the cottage. We had sown the seeds in September and transplanted the sturdy little plants in October. Now in January they were speedily climbing their supporting strings, and requiring the same persistent attention as painters give to the Forth Bridge.

They were scheduled to flower early in April; and we had chosen this crop, after earnest discussions with our horticultural advisers, because the greenhouse was unheated and sweet peas were certain to withstand the limited cold that might be expected in our area. We had not, however, foreseen the labour they would involve.

The shoots had endlessly to be pinched out, and when you have two thousand plants the extent of this mammoth task can become a nightmare. Not for Jane. She used to disappear into the greenhouse at eight o'clock in the morning and still be there at five in the evening, day after day. And when periodically I used to open the door and call for her, an answer would come from somewhere in the jungle of green like the squeak of a rabbit.

'Yes?'

'Are you all right?'

'Yes, thank you.'

I met her mother one day after a month of this and asked her how she thought Jane was enjoying herself. I felt sorry that her first task was proving so dull. It was very useful but dull.

'Oh,' said her mother, 'you don't have to worry. Do you know what she said to me yesterday? She said: "Mum, while I was among the sweet peas today I thought how lucky I was to be doing what I've wanted to do all my life."'

I believe one of the salutary first lessons I had was when I discovered that a task painstakingly performed did not inevitably result in achievement. It was a depressing discovery. Even as a boy I felt that the years were too short; and so when I learned one can often work arduously without at the end having anything to show, I was deeply affected. Ever since I have been impatient for quick results.

I wonder, then, if Jane was affected by what happened to the sweet peas. I do not expect so. The first disappointment does not do any harm. Only a scratch on the hand. It is hardly to be noticed. One is safe if there is no quick repetition; and then, when this happens, a girl like Jane will remorselessly struggle on to the next time. No doubts for her. Or, if there are, they are quelled.

Not a single sweet pea flowered. Not a bud. Not even

the prospect of a bloom, had we decided to continue nurturing the plants until Domesday. The leaves were a fine green and the stems thick as my little finger. No sign of disease. And Jane had attended to their wants, pinching the side shoots and performing the awkward, time-consuming, patience-testing task of layering ... she had cared for them with the same diligence as she would have cared for pampered children in a kindergarten. And now only foliage to gaze upon. Why?

I have had many inquests at Minack and doubtless will have many more. There is a macabre comfort in gathering together the specialists to stare at the doomed crop. One is paying court to the principle of learning from failure, and seeking reassurance that the catastrophe is not of one's own making.

And yet it can be a sterile experience. The specialists, spared of any financial interest, sometimes have a sadistic relish in declaring that if such and such had been done at such and such a time, all would have been well. It is their dogmatism that irks me. It is their forgetfulness. I have often been guided by specialists along paths which, after failure, they have forgotten were their idea.

So here we were staring gloomily at the sweet peas with a specialist. The curriculum began, as usual, with a few moments' silence, standing at the entrance of the greenhouse, the long lines of green offenders stretching in front of us. There followed a sudden movement, a few steps taken swiftly forward, a hand outstretched, a leaf rubbed between the fingers, a stem caressed, a finger poking at the soil around the roots; it was a ritual of cultural investigation I have witnessed many times before and since.

'What do you think?'

I maintain always a note of optimism in this question. Perhaps it springs from some primitive belief in the power of the witch-doctor; more likely it is a left-over hope from my youth in which the magic of the expert was daily drummed into me

'Get an expert's advice,' some relation would say to me comfortably. It is always a comfort to push a decision on to somebody else. It is pleasant to believe that there is *someone* who can answer your conundrum. It is security in an insecure world. It is the twentieth-century version of an aborigine's faith in an idol.

But there was, of course, nothing we could do about the sweet peas. Everyone agreed they were magnificent plants. Never before had it been known for such healthy specimens to be without flowers. It was extraordinary. It was worth making a special report. It was an example of what makes a specialist's life so interesting, a crop failure which defies interpretation. A crop failure. It happened to be the first crop we had grown in our splendid new greenhouse. And therein lay the clue to what had happened.

The site of the greenhouse was in the dip of the land in front of the cottage, and we had chosen it because we had no alternative. Our neighbour was still in possession of the flat fields which were more suitable; and we had no idea he was soon to leave and that we were to gain control of them. The site of the greenhouse had been a bog.

The bog had provided us with our first challenge at Minack. It had coaxed us into action because of the closely growing elm trees on three sides and the willow hedge, bordering the lane, on the other. Here was a haven for flowers, once we had succeeded in draining the water away.

It took three seasons to achieve. We began, in our foolishness, with a broken cup and a trowel, cutting little channels which had no effect on the bog whatsoever; and we ended up with hundreds of feet of earthenware drainpipes in three-foot-deep trenches and a deep gulley to rush the water away to the sea. Our reward was a good crop of violets one year, of anemones the next, of potatoes the third. And then we set our hearts on the greenhouse.

We were prompted, of course, by material reasons. We could not afford the capital expenditure, but we also could not afford to do without the income such capital expenditure might bring in. An old story. The lure that carefully planned extravagance reimburses the sacrifice it demands. The sheer necessity of adding to one's commitments in order to survive. The urge to lasso a future that only has optimism to guarantee success. Surely we are right to spend the money. Surely a greenhouse will be a fine investment.

We had drained the ground of surface water, but there was still the obstacle of three huge elms standing exactly in the middle of where the greenhouse would be. Why not a smaller greenhouse which would not interfere with the trees? Even the greenhouse salesman suggested it might be wiser if we were not so ambitious.

It was chilling to hear him trying to persuade us not to be so bold. We did not want to be bold ourselves. We would have preferred to change our minds; and yet there persisted a relentless gnawing inside us that we were on the right road. The rest of our lives was to be spent at Minack and nothing mattered, nothing at all, so long as we had the foundations which enabled us to exist. A small greenhouse demanded the same emotion to erect as a big one. The same worry. And as we could not even afford a small greenhouse, we would lose nothing by having a big one; irrational reasoning perhaps, but to us it made sense. For at least a big one would earn more money.

So instead of a fifty-foot house only ten foot wide, we ordered a hundred-foot house which was twenty foot wide; and the elms had to be removed.

I find it a little awesome when one puts in motion a large plan from which there is no turning back, and I was in this mood when I watched the end of the elms. It made me sensitive to the sadness of losing the trees. They had welcomed us when first we came to Minack, and I was now their executioner. I could not treat them briskly as inanimate objects which happened to bar my progress. They were entities of our life. I could not watch their end without sentiment. They had received our fresh eyes of enthusiasm and now were the victims of inescapable reality.

They were reluctant to go. I had engaged a young man to do the job who had arrived one day with a very old tractor and a saw. First the main branches were cut off each tree, then the main trunk just above

40

the base; and it was now that the elms became obstinate. A wire rope was lashed around the remains of the trunk and hitched to the tractor; and then the tractor was driven in short, quick bursts, so that the violence of its motion loosened the roots clinging deep to the soil. They were slow to loosen. I watched from the cottage window and was aware that any profit to the young man from the arrangement we had made together was likely to be dissipated by the break-up of his tractor.

'Listen,' I said to him, while he was having a particularly obstinate session with the last of the elms, 'let me find someone with a bulldozer.'

Such a foolish suggestion. The young man was a Cornishman who had intense belief in the value of being independent. Nobody was going to suggest he could not do a job. This was the kind of insult which reared angrily in a Cornishman's mind and remained there simmering long after everyone else had forgotten it. I had made a mistake and knew it as soon as I had spoken.

He and his tractor again attacked the old elm with venom, successfully removed it, and then he came politely to inform me that his activities had unearthed four large rocks exactly where the foundations of the new greenhouse would be.

'I'll remove them for you,' he said, looking at me carefully, 'if you want me to.'

I could not possibly say no; and as I gave him the go-ahead I had the coward's thought of wishing I had never embarked on the enterprise. I had started a chain of events which would carry me steadily forward, relentlessly as if I were an object on a conveyor belt. This greenhouse would be only a beginning. I would want more greenhouses. I was a man whose personal freedom depended upon twining more and more responsibilities around himself. I could not avoid them. If I were to maintain the momentum of our happiness at Minack, the fear of material failure had to accompany me and I had to learn to accept it. It was obvious I would be frightened when it was my nature to do nothing; but Jeannie and I were not a rich couple in their South of France villa lolling on the terrace wondering how to fill the day. We were escapists, but we were not escapists to idleness. We had to earn a living out of our personal endeavours; and I had to be prepared to brace myself against such fleeting fears as beset me that morning when I waited for the rocks to be jerked out of the places where they had been since the beginning of time.

I was helped by the attitude of the young man. I have often found that individuals who formed no part of my life have influenced me at crucial moments. I do not mean they have been aware that they have done so, nor that their influence has been on matters of much importance. But something they say or do reflects, it seems to me at the time, a part of me that I am searching for. I suddenly realise what it is I need.

For as I expected, the tractor broke down; but instead of bemoaning the fact, using it as an excuse to cease his task, the young man cheerfully said he would go off to find a spare part and would be back as quickly as possible. He had already snapped a wire rope, a rope which to this day lies on the hedge as a rusty memento of his efforts; and there were still two rocks to move. But back he came, and the tractor began roaring again, lunging angrily, anchored by the rock which moved only an inch at a time. I know now he was foolhardy and that the strain he imposed on the tractor was quite unnecessary; for a stone cutter would have split the rocks and they could have been dragged away easily in pieces. But at the time there was for me a shine in his obstinacy. I had someone to share my own.

The greenhouse, except for the foundations of cement and breeze blocks, arrived altogether on a lorry that edged down the lane with its cargo peering high above the hedge, the glass in vast packing cases, the cedarwood structure in numerous bundles. It was a terrifying sight. The lorry crept down the hill stopping every few yards halted by boulders on the edge of the lane which caught the wide wheels. It would back, the driver would twist his steering wheel, and then forward again, bumping and slithering towards Minack. It turned the last corner, straightened up for the last two hundred yards, and then I knew the really dangerous moment had arrived. A stretch lay ahead like a miniature causeway with a ditch on either side. Was it wide enough? Had we made a mistake when we built this part of the lane?

For this lorry, in a fashion, was making a maiden voyage. Only a few weeks before, the lane had been changed from the appearance of the dried-up bed of a turbulent river, into a surface fit for a limousine. Up until then we had called it our chastity belt. It had been impassable for private cars and rough enough for the Land Rover to make us hesitate to go out on trivial errands. We had been contained in a world of our own choosing, voluntary prisoners whose object was to be screened from the kind of life we had left.

The idea of building the lane did not mean our attitude had changed. We were as immune from gregariousness as when we first arrived. We saw no gain in transferring ourselves from a city social life of which we had grown tired into a countrified version with its added drawbacks. At least in a city your attendance at a party is mitigated by the probable proximity of your hosts; in the country you have to develop the habit of driving forty miles there and back. Our life was too full for such waste of time. We were content in each other's company.

We decided to build the lane because we realised it was necessary for our business. We could hardly expect to be treated seriously by salesmen who had to leave their cars a quarter of a mile away from us. We could sense in their manner on arrival at the cottage that they labelled us as amateurs; which we were, of course, but not in the way that they inferred. We were not playing at growing as they hinted. We were so painfully serious that we were touchy.

This touchiness came to boiling point one day when an official called on behalf of the Ministry of Agriculture to investigate our qualifications for a road-building grant. This grant, which meant that fifty per cent of the cost would be paid for by the Ministry, was obviously vital to our plans; and when, through the sitting room window, I saw the official arrive, I determined to be on my best behaviour. Here was an occasion when I must not display my allergy to officialdom.

He wore a smart tweed cap, a check flannel shirt, a bow tie, and a loosely cut country suit, the uniform of a prosperous farmer on market day. He was indeed a farmer, one who was engaged by the Ministry to serve on Agricultural Committees that watched over the affairs of fellow farmers. An unpaid job. An over-worked one. But one which carried with it the pleasures of prestige.

I came out of the cottage and down the sloping path to where he was standing, a smile on my face and my hand outstretched.

'Good afternoon,' I said warmly, 'it's very nice of you to come.'

I had scarcely uttered these words when I sensed he did not wish to notice my arrival. He was gazing round at the broken-down walls, the shells of disused buildings of long ago. He threw a glance at the cottage. He stared across the untidy moorland to the sea. He looked at some boulders heaped on one side of the path. It was obvious he was performing an act for my benefit.

'Gosh,' he suddenly said, 'What a place!' And had I looked close enough I would have seen him shudder.

I knew at once what he was up to. The Ministry quite rightly had to guard against unwarranted claims as there were, in any case, enough genuine claims to soak up the grant allocations. Hence it was perhaps inevitable that people like ourselves were looked upon with suspicion; for we might be pretending to have a market garden in order to gain the advantage of the grant.

'Good afternoon,' I repeated. But I no longer offered my hand. Whatever his suspicions he had no need to be tough.

'Don't tell me you live here all the year round?'

He had addressed me for the first time, looking me up and down as he did so, as if he were judging the points of a steer. I felt uncomfortable.

'Yes, indeed,' I said, keeping my voice calm, 'it is the most wonderful place in the world.'

I was rather like a father whose child has been unfairly criticised. Here was our beloved Minack receiving the scorn of a stranger. Our life was being questioned. Someone who did not know anything about us was daring to suggest to my face that Minack was not a fit place to live in. My touchiness was awake. His attitude could not have been better calculated to make me lose my temper.

'You had better show me round,' he said.

It was February and in Minack fields the green shoots of the early potatoes were breaking through the ground. Down the cliff the haulms were already beginning to cover the rows; and over at Pentewan the two acres of meadows we rented were a picture of possible prosperity. Facing due south and earlier than Minack they had long rows of youthful potato tops, a foot apart, lines of healthy, dark green; and we were very proud of them.

'I don't see how you can expect to get a potato crop from *this* meadow.'

The tour, I had expected, would prove to the official that we were, after all, serious growers. We had seven tons of seed potatoes. We were one of the largest growers of cliff early potatoes west of Penzance. And I confidently felt, as we set out, that the official would quench his asperity as soon as he took stock of our efforts. Now he was criticising the condition of a meadow; and the maddening thing was he was right. We had happened to pass the one meadow at Pentewan of which I was not proud. It was patchy. It needed weeding. But what was it to do with him?

I am one of those who have never felt comfortable in the possession of power over a fellow human being. It is my weakness of character that I can never give an order or attempt to impose my will without a wavering doubt. I do not want to hurt. I do not want to exploit the weakness of another because I am aware of the weakness in myself. I could never become a tin god because I have never believed that the pursuit of power is an end in itself.

Such an attitude, however, breeds on occasion a violent reaction. The easy way out of letting things slide, the lack of courage or conviction to state your views clearly suddenly comes up against a brick wall; for suddenly some incident, on top of all those others you have failed to face up to, stings you into fury. You explode, and the victim is surprised. He has underestimated you.

The official, of course, was surprised when I

exploded. I put up for an hour with his taunts and then could not restrain myself any longer. My politeness suddenly turned into rage. The anger which I had felt as soon as I first saw him had simmered into an outburst in which my words tumbled out so fast that they stumbled over each other. I finished by saying:

'And anyway, what damn right have you got to speak to me like this? I'm asking for a grant, not a lecture!'

He was amazed. It was as if a gale had blown him fiat. He grinned at me sheepishly. He fingered the peak of his cap and shuffled his foot round an imaginary stone. I was amused to see how suddenly he had become deflated.

'Now, now, now,' he said soothingly, 'I didn't mean to sound rude. I've a difficult job to do. I can't recommend grants for everybody. I must make sure . . . I promise I will do my best in your case.'

We shook hands after that.

And we secured our grant.

The lorry was now advancing on the trickiest part of the lane. The miniature causeway covered the section which was filled with quickthorn and elm tree saplings when we first came to Minack; and in the winter it used to become a swamp, collecting the water which drained down the valley. Hence the contractor whom we employed to build the lane raised up this section, leaving ditches on either side to act as drains. There was not an inch to spare. The driver had to keep the wheels plumb straight or else the lorry with its enormous load, a load of such high hopes for Jeannie and myself, would topple over.

Slowly, slowly . . . it was now halfway across and I could see the driver in the cabin grimly holding the steering wheel. Never had a greenhouse been delivered in such dangerous circumstances. Why on earth was I courting disaster? This was only the beginning. Had not somebody warned me that a greenhouse would never stand up to the gales that lashed Minack?

'Come on, come on.'

I was standing a few yards in front of the bonnet. I could see the fat tyres of the back wheels riding the lane's edges as if on two tightropes. Another three feet . . .

The lorry was safe.

It took a fortnight to erect the greenhouse; and when it was completed Jeannie and I used to stand inside for an hour on end, gazing in wonderment. It was our personal Crystal Palace. The expanse of it, the heat of the sunshine despite the cold winds outside, the prospect of now being able to grow crops without the endless threat of the elements, produced such excitement that we bought a bottle of champagne and christened it.

'To the greenhouse and its crops!' And we stood in the middle with glasses raised.

It was a pity, therefore, that the sweet peas behaved as they did. With such a beginning they might have responded by flowering. Even a few flowers.

But we did not know that sweet pea plants become sterile if the roots are in wet soil; because that winter, while we proudly watched the lush green climbing up the strings, the roots had found their way to the drainpipes.

And so our first crop had been doomed before it started to grow.

Hubert when he was king of the roof

4

In the summer Jane once again disappeared into the greenhouse, tending the tomatoes.

We had seven hundred plants of a variety called Moneymaker in eight long rows. Each had a string attached, like the sweet peas, around which the stem had to be twisted as the plant grew; and each had to have their shoots continually pinched out so that the main stem was left to grow on its own. Then at a later stage the plants were defoliated.

It was easy to teach Jane what to do. As with Shelagh, Jeannie or I had only to show her something once for her to grasp the idea, and probably improve on it. She watched plants, any plants she was looking after, as if they were individuals; and so if a tomato plant, for instance, showed signs of a fault, she was quick to notice it.

'Mr Tangye?'

'Yes, Jane?'

I would be standing at the greenhouse door and from somewhere in the green foliage in front of me piped her small voice.

'The thirty-first plant in the third row from the right shows signs of botrytis on its stem.'

Sometimes I have noticed among people who work on market gardens a certain pleasure in reporting some disease or other misfortune to a crop. Not so Jane. I always found she was as upset as myself that something was wrong.

When it was fine she worked barefooted, looking like a child peasant, blue jeans and loose shirt, with the summer sun bleaching her hair fairer and fairer. There was something of a pagan about her. She was unlike Shelagh, who was to be as tidy at the end of the day as at the beginning, however dirty the work she had been doing. Instead Jane, within an hour of arriving, would have smudges on her face which would remain there until she went home. She was quite unconcerned.

It was particularly dirty among the tomato plants, and so Jane was an inevitable victim. Tomato plants ooze a green stain-like dye. I had only to walk the length of the greenhouse between two rows for my shirt to be touched with green. And so Jane, who spent the whole day there, would finish up with green hands, a green face and, for that matter, green hair.

She had an unreliable sense of time. Both her mother and herself had a strange effect on watches. I believe this sometimes happens when people have a surfeit of electricity in their bodies; but whatever the reason no watch would keep correct time for these two. Hence Jane would occasionally arrive for work at unconventional hours. Sometimes very early, sometimes very late.

Of course, it did not matter her being late because she could make up the time at the end of the day. Indeed, she was never a clock-watcher. She always stayed on until the job was finished. But in the beginning, when she was late, when she did not know what our reaction might be, she used to creep along like a Red Indian, keeping out of sight behind hedges, reaching Minack by a roundabout route; and hoping that she could begin work without her absence having been noted. She did it out of adventure, not out of guile. She always told us in the end.

At first we used to water the tomato plants in the old-fashioned way with a hose; and it was Jane's job to spend hour after hour dragging the length of the hose down the path behind her, thrusting the nozzle towards the base of the plants on either side. Jane performed the boring task without complaint but when I, at week-ends, took her place, I soon found myself wondering why I should waste my time in such a way. My time, and Jane's, could be better employed doing something else.

So here was the old evergreen problem. Money had to be spent to save money. Sense seemed to be on the side of extravagance for if the watering was made auto-matic not only would hours be saved, but also it would be distributed more accurately. The arguments seemed wonderfully convincing. My only hesitation sprang from my impatience that the price of efficiency should be a bottomless pit.

I always hesitate. I have never bought a piece of horticultural equipment with the élan that others, for instance, buy a car they cannot afford. I never enjoy that feeling of wild abandon that comes to people who have had a burst of extravagance. I have been extravagant, I have spent money I cannot spare, but the equipment which is the result gives me no joy. Its only attraction is its necessity.

Salesmen are quickly aware of my lack of enthusiasm so they tempt me by the hook of sound sense. As I am not buying for pleasure, as I look as if I am the gloomiest buyer imaginable, they set out to pierce my resistance by likening the piece of offered equipment to someone I might be employing. It is a persuasive trick.

'Now if you pay £12 a month for this tractor you can't say that's an agricultural wage,' a salesman will say to me, 'and yet you'll have a machine doing five times an ordinary man's work in a week. Five times? . . . I should have said twenty times!

'And the money paid to a workman is gone . . . you'll never see it again. Look at it this way . . . you pay the hire-purchase as if it's a wage. Then . . .' and this was always the telling moment in the sales talk . . . 'then in twelve months you've got a workman for free!'

I have fallen so often for this patter. It subtly appeals to my progressive ambitions. It even suggests that I am getting something for nothing. So I yield. And as a result I have had many an inanimate workman at Minack on hire-purchase pay rolls. The automatic irrigation was to be another.

It consisted of rubber tubing, the thickness of my forefinger, which ran the length of the greenhouse alongside the base of each row of plants. Opposite each plant was a nozzle and, when the tap was turned on, all the plants began to receive by drips an equal amount of water.

It had a still further advantage. The top end of the tubes was connected to a larger tube which, in turn, was hitched to the water tap; but, and this was the cunning part, the tube on its way to the tap was fastened to a contraption in a two-gallon glass jar. In this jar was tomato feed concentrate, and by turning the dial on the contraption, one could control the feed for the plants as soon as the tap was turned on. It could be a strong feed or a weak feed, and all the plants got the same.

Such standardised feeding naturally contains certain snags. Not all the plants have the same appetites, nor do they desire identical meals; some want more nitrogen than others, some more potash. But I have learned now to forget the odd men out. If the bulk is all right, and I now grow thousands of plants, I am only too thankful that I have an inanimate workman to look after them.

The water came from the well up the lane, a surface well that now belonged to us. This water was unsuitable, as far as we were concerned, for human consumption; and so we continued to use the well above the cottage, which we sank ourselves, for domestic purposes.

This well remains a shining example of how expensive it can be if you set out to do a thing cheaply. I had been assured that the spring lay so near the surface that it would cost only £30 to reach it. I watched the £30 disappear, and saw no sign that the hole was even damp. I should, of course, have cut my losses and fetched the firm who find water by boring a hole. But their charges at the time seemed enormous. I was not impressed by their guarantee of a huge column of water. I could not afford to be.

Instead I urged the two miners I had engaged from the mines at St Just to dig on. And on and on they dug. It was a beautiful hole, if a hole in the ground can be beautiful, the sides plumb straight, the granite sliced like a knife by their skilful hand-drilling and dynamiting; but never a sign of water. The hole was so deep that I dared not stop. So much of my money was now down the hole that it was too late to seek the help of the others. Perhaps another foot, or another, or another . . .

My persistency never gained its true reward. The miners got thirty feet down then a man with a compressor and special drilling equipment tried drilling twenty-foot holes. Water was found in the end; but it was a lazy trickle of water taking its time to fill the bottom of the well. It still takes its time. And in October, when springs fall low, it can only pump seventy gallons before it is dry.

Our tomatoes, therefore, were dependent on the well up the lane; and we were lucky to secure the water without the expense of pumping for it. The reason was simple, though, to my kind of mind, it was difficult to understand. It was a question of gravity. The well up the lane was so much higher than the level of the greenhouse that, having dropped a copper pipe with perforated holes in the well and then, patiently filled the alkathene pipe between the well and the greenhouse with water, a stream came out of the tap by the greenhouse like a main.

It was not, however, always as clean as a main. This did not matter because part of the equipment for the automatic irrigation was a filter and this prevented even the smallest build-up of dirt from blocking the nozzles attending each plant. But the filter, of course, had periodically to be cleaned.

I noticed, however, in late June of this particular

summer, that Jane was spending an inordinate amount of time attending to this filter. I could not feel such attention was justified; I liked Jane very much but I could not allow her to dally. I was particularly irked when I saw she was emptying the dirt from the filter into the pail. This was really foolish. I could not understand how she could justify her time in doing this. The filter needed only be rinsed. There was nothing more to it than that.

It was not so important that I had to make a fuss. Indeed it was only when I was in a worrying mood that I thought anything about it. She worked hard enough. If she slipped up by being slow on the filter, it balanced all the other good work she did. It was trivial. It was one of those small situations which only erupt when a boss seeks a quarrel.

'What are you doing, Jane?'

It was just before the lunch hour, and I happened to pass Jane as she, barefooted, was bending earnestly over both filter and pail. She looked up at me so freshly, having noticed no note in my voice to suggest that, in reality, I was vexed with her, and said:

'I'm rescuing the tadpoles.'

Then, of course, I saw what was happening. The suction of the pipe in the well up the lane was sucking the tadpoles, which abounded at that time of the year in the well, into the pipe which led to the greenhouse; and quickly, they were blocking the filter. Jane, having discovered what was happening, served both the tomato plants by cleaning the filter and the tadpoles by returning them to the well.

'I take them up in my lunch hour back to the well,'

she said timidly, yet with a tiny note of defiance, 'or at the end of the day.' She had put them, of course, in the pail. That was how she was spending her time when she prompted my doubt about her. What could I say?

I was down on my knees beside her before I spoke. A tadpole, still alive, was clutched to the face of the filter, and Jane, with a stalk of couch grass, was easing it away. It was flabby. A tiny piece of flabbiness that, to rescue, would make all the clever people laugh. It was a thing alive, but why help it? What a strange waste of time to find pleasure in an object so unproductive. And yet this was the kind of pleasure that was the pulse of mankind, the creed of those who prefer to face the present rather than scurry away.

'My dear Jane,' I said in a very practical manner, 'I'm all in favour of you helping the tadpoles . . . but they'll only come back again through the pipe.'

She glanced up at me, just a flash, as if I were an ignorant man.

'Only a few,' she said, 'the others will be safe.' Then she grinned, looking up at me as if she had known all the time what I had been thinking, making me feel foolish, 'I'll be working an extra half-hour today!'

We had a wonderful crop of tomatoes that summer, and Jeannie and I were quick to realise that the success was a signpost to the future. We still grew potatoes on a large scale, but here was an alternative for a summer income which did not suffer the everlasting threat of obliteration by the elements. I saw too another particular advantage. Tomatoes and potatoes are of the same family, and if our district was noted for the earliness of the potatoes, it could also be noted for the earliness of the tomatoes; and earliness, of course, meant a chance of higher prices. Furthermore there was not the expense of sending the crop to distant markets. We could sell every tomato we picked in Penzance. The vast influx of holiday-makers were waiting to eat them.

We put in the plants, that first year, in the beginning of April, and by the middle of June they were a festoon of ripening fruit. We began to have visitors. Word had got around among neighbouring farmers of our good fortune and, although they would never grow a tomato themselves, they could not forbear to investigate the extent of our success. It was a relief to us that we had something so pleasant to show them. It was a change. Instead of insecurely seeking their advice I was able to talk to them on a subject they knew nothing about. Of course, I knew little myself, and I am not much wiser even now; but I have learned certain principles which now set the pace of our growing at Minack.

It is no use growing our own plants from seed because too much time and labour are involved. Seedlings require the art of the expert and in my case, as far as we were concerned, they take up space in a greenhouse just at the period when we need that space for the winter flower crop. It is more profitable, therefore, to collect cash for the flowers and pay out cash for the plants.

But this policy is not as straightforward as it sounds. If we grew our own plants they would be there on the premises to plant out in their permanent positions whenever it happened to suit us. We could delay or hasten the planting out according to the progress of the winter flowers; if the flowers, freesias, for instance, were still blooming and fetching a good price, we could hold back the tomatoes for a week or so. If, because of a warm spring, the flowers finished early, the tomatoes could be planted early. We would, in fact, be independent.

As it is we are at the mercy of whoever it is we have asked to supply us. We order the plants before Christmas, state a guesswork of a date when we will want them, then are ready to accept the panic which is sure to beset us. It is not only the progress of our flowers that we have to worry about; we can also expect the supplier suddenly to disrupt our carefully laid plans by saying he is delivering the plants a week early, or for that matter, it could equally be a week later.

Thus from the middle of March to the beginning of April every year I am generally in a state of high excitement. I am not alone. Tomato growers all over the country are also yelping cries of distress. Shall we scrap the flowers, which are still earning us money? If we don't, where can we put the tomatoes in the mean-time? Don't you realise they'll get leggy if we put the soil blocks too close? Surely it's wiser to look after the tomatoes from the beginning?

When the turmoil is over and the plants are in the ground, there begins a pleasant period of observation. The period in which the little plants create pleasure by the sturdy way they show they accept their new quarters. It is now that Jeannie and I will waste time together in the greenhouse, staring fixedly at the plants and making remarks to each other such as:

'They're an awfully good colour.'

'That one over there has a flower already.'

'Hello, there's one with stem rot.'

'Don't tell me that's a Moneymaker. It's a rogue.'

As they develop, as they progress from the innocent stage of lining the greenhouse in straight rows like guardsmen on parade, both Jeannie and I become more suspicious.

'Am I imagining it? But some look like missing their first truss.'

'Why is it that every year that patch on the left, half-way down, has such a pale green?'

'I don't know, Jeannie, but some of these stems seem a little thin. I'll start feeding.'

It is wonderful the various ways that one can be advised how to grow a good crop of tomatoes. So many experts, never lacking assurance, pronounce what the grower ought to do. Some, for example, say you should begin feeding as soon as the plants have been planted. Others, that you must let a plant struggle to establish itself; a kind of test of character suggesting that plants are like students. The diet is equally perplexing.

As a matter of convenience we fed the tomatoes that first year with a concoction having the title of Orange Ring. We read, however, in an article in the trade press, that this was a lazy way of feeding; and as we were amateurs desperately anxious to grow the right way we duly took note of what we ought to have done. At successive stages of growth we should have given them Red Ring, Orange Ring, Blue Ring, and finished up with Green Ring; and technically speaking this meant that they begin with a high amount of potash and ended with a high amount of nitrogen. Can you imagine our confusion then, when the following year the pontification was reversed? And that we were right in the first place? That Orange Ring fed all the way through the season had now been proved to give the best results?

But now it is the end of June and we are beginning to pick; and Jane has emerged from the green forest with a basket of tomatoes in either hand and with the news that she has only picked a single row.

'There are masses in there,' she says excitedly, 'absolutely masses.'

It is a sweet moment when a long-awaited harvest awakes. It shares the common denominator of pleasure which embraces all endeavours that have taken a long time to plan, to nurture, and then suddenly bursts before your eyes in achievement. You are no longer an onlooker waiting impatiently. The harvest is there to give you your reward; the fact of it destroys your worries and galvanises you into action. I know of few things so evergreen sweet as the first picking of a new crop.

But mine, as far as the tomatoes were concerned, was only a token picking. It was Jeannie and Jane who disappeared into the greenhouse twice a week; and then Shelagh too when she came to work for us and we had the additional greenhouses. I was considered too clumsy. It was alleged that I carelessly knocked the trusses as I passed down the rows, knocking off tomatoes before they were ripe, stepping on and squashing them as they lay on the soil. It was pleasant for them to have a butt.

'He's an elephant, isn't he, Mrs Tangye?'

'Elephants should be more careful.'

A pause for a few moments as the picking continued. Then a small voice and a giggle.

'Oh, well, some jobs men will never do as well as women.'

I was, therefore, in charge of taking the tomatoes to the packing shed, grading and packing them, then driving the chips to Penzance. Each full chip, of course, weighed twelve pounds and I separated them into two grades; normal-sized tomatoes, then misshapen and small ones together. Such straightforward grading is, however, considered a sin. The cry is for perfect uniformity. The perfect chip of tomatoes, in the opinion of the leaders of the industry, is one that contains fruit of exactly the same shape, as if the contents have been churned out of a machine.

Flavour, it seems, does not matter; the tomato can taste of nothing at all and still win the laurels. Perfect shape, perfect size, but it can taste of soap; and this campaign of artificial standards is considered essential if the needs of the housewife are to be met. Who is this palateless housewife? No doubt a computer-produced automaton.

Thus I continue to grade on the basis that people still want tasty tomatoes and therefore, within reason, the shape and size are unimportant. And yet how much longer will I be able to do this? I grow a tomato variety which is bred to have flavour. The thousands and thousands of tons of tomatoes which are shipped into this country every year have only shape as their merit.

These varieties produce more tomatoes per plant and can be sold cheaper. It therefore may be only a question of time before, I too, sell tasteless tomatoes.

When you have a crop such as tomatoes which you sell locally, it is tempting to bypass the wholesaler and court the retailers and hotels instead. In theory it is a splendid idea. You will obviously get a better price. But there are snags in the theory which Jeannie and I soon found out when we tried this method of sales ourselves.

To begin with we had the wrong temperaments. We could not bargain. We could not say to a retailer: 'The price is so much.' Instead we would arrive at the shop and timidly ask what price they could give us which would allow them a profit. We were not in command. We were supplicants. And if indeed they expressed a desire for so many chips on the following Friday, on the preceding Thursday we would take so much time selecting the tomatoes that it would have been more profitable from a man-hour point of view to have sold them at half the price elsewhere.

As for hotels, they provided us with a subtle danger. If I were leaning against a bar having a pint, and the landlord asked for three chips next Saturday morning, I would of course have to say I would deliver them. The landlord would infer he was doing me a favour by helping me to dispose of my produce.

But Saturday would come, and being in a peaceful mood, the last thing I then wanted was to drive to Penzance. The chips of tomatoes, however, were promised. I had to take them. I was in business, and I would be collecting sixpence a pound more than I would have done at a wholesaler. Eighteen shillings, in fact, for the three chips.

The cost of the Land Rover at a shilling a mile was ten shillings; and so, from an accountant's point of view, I now had eight shillings left as a profit.

That, unfortunately, was not the end of my expenses. Having come into Penzance with the tomatoes in a mood of duty instead of pleasure, it did not take much persuasion to stay a little longer than I had planned. A little longer than both of us had planned.

Because Jeannie and I always went together unless there was a specific reason not to do so. Neither of us has ever developed the habit of going out on our own. Jeannie had never shown any inclination to take part in gatherings of her sex, while I have never discovered the advantage of spending a session in men's company at the expense of leaving her at home. And so when tomatoes were to be delivered at a hotel I would always hope that Jeannie would come with me.

We would arrive and the landlord would offer us a drink. A little later, when he had paid me, I would offer him one in return. And now would begin the rising of our *alter egos,* the egos which were occasionally waiting to beckon us back to the life we used to know. We began to enjoy ourselves. We became careless and forgetful. And so it was not until we returned to Minack, bumping down the lane to the cottage, that we remembered our tomato profit had been dissipated. Nothing had been gained except the anger of time wasted, nothing achieved except a limpid imitation of a life of which we had grown tired. The tomatoes embroiled us. It would be safer to deal through a wholesaler.

I first met my wholesaler when I was walking down Market Jew Street and a voice shouted at me, aggressive, but friendly:

'When are we going to do business?'

The voice, in fact, belonged to half my wholesaler, to George, the Jackson brother with a handlebar moustache. He and his brother Harold had built up from a borrowed five-pound note a chain of retail greengrocery shops in West Cornwall, apart from a wholesale business in the area served by lorries.

So I began sending them potatoes, then crates of lettuce, and in due course, they began receiving all our tomatoes. We committed our produce entirely to them. We neither sought other outlets or argued about the price. It was as if, having endured the stresses of growing, we had no energy left to cosset the produce on its final stage. Thus as time went by they became a barometer of our progress. They were always fair.

'Easing up on potatoes, aren't you? Wise, old man, you're wise.'

'Been a good lettuce year for you. I've been looking at the figures.'

'Take my tip, get your tomatoes *early*.'

Periodically, as growers always do with their wholesalers, I would have a token row with them. I would find the dark, handsome Harold, who looked like a Guards officer, standing at the entrance of the warehouse that was close to the harbour. I would fume at him for some low price I had received, and he would reply by blinding me with figures as to why I was lucky to get any price at all. And if I were in the mood to be dispassionate I would see the truth of what he said.

'Absolute glut of tomatoes, old man. Turning them away. What can one do when Jerseys are selling at sixpence a pound?'

It is at such moments that I have a despair that seems to freeze me with fear. There has to be behind any endeavour a façade of confidence which the individual concerned is aware is pretence. This make-believe confidence is the propulsion which drives you to the success you aim for. But it is a frail thing. If you talk loud enough, if nobody contradicts you so vehemently that you have to listen, if you meet with no unfair disaster, then you can nose this confidence until you reach a harbour.

But I was a long way from harbour. I could not fall back, shrugging my shoulders and saying to Jeannie, 'Oh, well, it's just one of those seasons.'

Because when Harold Jackson told me that day there was a glut, it happened to be our first summer of tomatoes. The greenhouse had been erected almost a year. First we had the failure of the sweet peas; and now the superb crop of tomatoes, clustering like huge grapes from the stems, had met a glut.

I was frightened at that moment in a base way. I wanted to give up. I felt that if after all the thought we had given to our future, if after all the strain of raising the money for our plans, if after all the denial of personal pleasures in order to consolidate our present, we were to be defeated again by circumstances beyond our control, surely it would be wisest to surrender.

This was an occasion when, if a partner of an enterprise snares the other into sharing his weakness, the brave hopes dissolve. I tried to ensnare Jeannie.

She would not allow me to.

5

I wonder sometimes which of the Walter Mittys in me I was looking for. It is easy to become so immersed in day-to-day events that you lose sight of yourself. It is a chronic disease. A daze of living. The twentieth century speeds faster and faster and the pace only allows you to live in perpetual disguise.

But I had time of my own. In the matter of motion it would seem I belonged to another age. I had the sumptuous daily experience of getting up in the morning when I wanted to get up, not because I feared a factory hooter or the punishing look of an office doorkeeper. I could lie on the rocks on a sunny winter's day staring at the sea, while others could only peruse a brochure for next summer's fortnight. I seemed to be as free as anyone can be in a brittle society; and yet I was looking for a Walter Mitty.

I still do not know which one it was I wanted to be. I do not believe it was ever clear in my mind. I had only the wish to survive, to preserve our way of life at Minack at any cost; and if this meant behaving in a manner utterly opposite to the intentions with which we began, it had to be accepted as the penalty of personal freedom.

Perhaps in my subconscious I have always wanted to be a tycoon, and a tycoon was my Walter Mitty. Certainly in my limited way I behaved like one. Within the next two years I had bought a tractor, a large number of daffodil bulbs, and four more greenhouses.

I was consumed by the conviction that our business could only be made successful by capital expenditure; and as that capital, like the capital of most businesses, could only be borrowed, the noose was tightening around my neck. The more I extended my plans, the more committed I became to responsibilities I wanted to avoid. I was pursuing the age-old formula of sacrificing the present for the ephemeral future. I had to spend in order to earn the turnover which would give us security.

Our fourteen acres stretched along the rim of Mount's Bay, glorious meadows tilting towards the sea where we could stand and marvel at the beauty of the fishing boats below us as they hurried busily east to Newlyn and west towards Land's End. And beyond were the cargo boats and Atlantic liners sailing aslant across the horizon from the Wolf Rock to the Lizard.

The gannets dived a half-mile out, sometimes singly, sometimes by the score, plummeting from the sky, hitting the water with a spit of a bullet. The gulls fluttered low, watching as if enviously. Cormorants sped on their mysterious missions. Curlews called their wistful cries. And sometimes as we stood there the sea looked so meek that it seemed there never would be a storm again; and sometimes its rage was so terrible that we held each other and were scared.

In olden days most of this land was cared for by hand labour. The meadows were too confined and steep for a plough, and so the shovels used to lurch through the soil. They were being used on this land when we first came to Minack, but I, thinking of myself as forward-looking, decided I could do the work both more cheaply and more efficiently by using machines. Hence I began using a rotovator.

It was a punishing instrument; and after three or four hours of hurtling up and down the meadows clutching its handlebars, I used to return to the cottage and lie down exhausted on the sofa. Nor did my muscles ever learn to accept the punishment, and for days following a rotovating session I would ache with muscular pains.

It was never a friendly machine. It was obstinate to start, drawing the fire of my temper even before the real task had begun. It broke down with frequency, as if it were a recalcitrant workman who pursued a policy of lightning strikes whenever he considered the work was too tough for him. It was dangerous. Once it turned over, a tine hooking my foot as it did so, and putting me to bed for a fortnight. I hated it, and although there would always be periods when it would be useful, I had to face up to the fact that it was too small for the job we now had in hand; and in any case, having suffered so much myself I could hardly expect Geoffrey, who now worked for me, to suffer as well.

We set about, therefore, searching for a tractor. It had to be small and easily manoeuvrable, and it most certainly had to be well balanced. Tractors are inclined to topple over on any hilly ground, but at Minack a tractor would face tests like those of a motorbike scramble. We perused the catalogues, Geoffrey and I, and decided that two might meet our requirements; and we asked for a demonstration. Each tractor came from rival firms. Both arrived at the same time.

It was a cold November afternoon and an east wind from the sea was chilling our fields. A cheerless day and its mood fitted that of the demonstrators. They were irritated they had chosen the same hour to show off their paces. They eyed each other, coat collars buttoned high, as if they were rival centurions waiting for the off in their chariots.

I sensed that both were apprehensive. This was no ordinary demonstration in which the trial tractor patrolled an inoffensive field, careering up and down like a new car on a highway. It was like the course for an obstacle race. Steep slopes, hidden rocks just below the surface of the ground, tablecloth spaces to turn upon . . . all these lay ahead. It amused me to observe Geoffrey, who had planned the course, wryly smiling in the background as the first tractor set out for the start.

It was a crawler. A small track-propelled tractor, based on a tank. It was also, as far as Geoffrey and I had secretly decided, the favourite. There was something secure about a tractor without wheels, crawling along with its whole body on the ground. A sudden bump could not upset it as a rock might upset a wheel. It moved relentlessly clasping the soil so that, if the chance were there, it would climb up a mountain. We had read these things in the catalogue. We watched it set off.

The demonstrator, perched in the seat, was accompanied by two city-dressed colleagues. The presence of these two served, perhaps, as a moral support; but they looked cold, and unsure of their duties, and I could not help feeling that within minutes of arriving at Minack they fervently wished they had never come.

It so happened that Jeannie, without my having to say anything, felt exactly the same; and she arrived just as the demonstration was about to begin with a jug of tea. I wonder how many jugs of tea Jeannie has brewed for no other reason than that she hoped to give somebody confidence. Anyhow, after the tea, the crawler set off on the first test set by Geoffrey, and the two city-dressed gentlemen walked along by its side offering directions.

Unfortunately these directions were necessary. I was aware within a few minutes of the operation beginning that the crawler had never been designed for such deceit of the earth as awaited it at Minack. The first test was a level piece of ground called from time immemorial the stable field; and Geoffrey had chosen it as a limber-up. It appeared so simple that he had considered it a kindness that the first trip of both machines should plough such a level surface.

After five yards the crawler came suddenly to a stop, as if it had been a yacht in full sail which had been jerked immovable by an anchor. The two gentlemen gathered round the demonstration; and I observed that the other, the rival demonstrator, showed his good manners by turning his back on them and walking away. There was a flurry of instructions and counter instructions, then the two gentlemen, their faces pink with cold, backed away as if they were the seconds of a boxer in the ring; and the crawler started off again. Another jerk. Another full stop.

As I watched, Geoffrey beside me, I had a strange premonition that it was I, not the tractor, who was running into trouble. I found myself thinking, affected no doubt by the bleakness of the afternoon, that it was unreal that the people present were dependent in some form on my patronage; the demonstrators who would have their reports to make, success or failure to explain; Geoffrey who would be passing on his observations over high tea at home; and even Jane, though not directly concerned, would go back across the fields at five and discuss the events of the afternoon with her mother. None of these people would have been at Minack were it not for Jeannie and me, and the dreams we had. And now they were leading me, almost dragging me along a route which frightened me.

For I could not pretend I had any lilt in deciding which tractor to buy. The acquisition would be a burden. There would be no prospect of some light-hearted compensation. It was not a foolish venture of frivolous intent. It was utilitarian. A lump of metal which would remind me day after day of the penalties of expansion. I was standing there, the wind sharp against my face, being courted by an object I did not want; which would prove irresistible. I was at a beginning that had no banners to welcome me. I had no feeling of faith, as I watched, that what I was doing, what I was prepared to gamble, what

74

indeed were my secret hopes . . . that any of these things were justified. I was being driven by a force that did not belong to me, which I distrusted, yet obeyed.

I watched the crawler fail, and had this stupid, maddening premonition that it was the symbol of my own failure. I was trying to be too big, entering a realm in which my nature did not belong; as if I were thrusting myself on a social scene which did not intend to receive me. I was taking on the outward appearance of a go-getter without possessing the inward equipment, the standard of ruthlessness, the lack of sentiment, the greed masquerading in the guise of efficiency. I was trying to play a role for which I had no heart and to adopt characteristics which I had escaped to Minack to avoid. I felt frightened of myself on that unfriendly November afternoon. Yet I had to make a decision.

I bought the second tractor; and Geoffrey was as pleased as I was doubtful. It was an odd-looking machine, the diesel engine was behind the driving seat and the instruments were placed in the centre between the four wheels. These instruments, the plough, for instance, were controlled by hydraulic lifts with levers fixed to the steering-wheel column for the use of the driver. Thus, if you were ploughing, you unhitched a lever and the plough dropped to the ground and off it went turning its furrow as soon as you put the tractor in gear. Then you pulled the lever in the opposite direction and up came the plough clear of the ground. This system had for us great advantages. The driver could watch the plough at work below him, and so had an admirable chance to nose the plough without mishap over the numerous rocks which hid just beneath the surface of the soil. But there were rocks above the ground, and the steepness of the meadows; and from the beginning I was scared by the devil-may-care attitude that Geoffrey adopted to these hazards.

'For heaven's sake, Jeannie,' I would shout, 'look at Geoffrey!' And Geoffrey would be careering over one of the larger meadows as if the tractor were a racing car.

Indeed from the beginning Geoffrey behaved to the tractor as if it were his own. He was for ever polishing, oiling, greasing, testing the tyres, and taking it out of the shelter where it was kept on any pretext he could devise. It was his toy, and I was not allowed to interfere.

'What are you doing this morning, Geoffrey?'

'Ploughing the sol meadow.'

I was stimulated to find him so keen. I was also apprehensive.

'Be careful.'

I was apprehensive not only because he drove the tractor fast, but also because he seemed to have no fear in its handling. He would, for instance, be ready to plough a steep meadow *uphill;* and the engine being at the rear, the tractor was then poised to turn turtle. I used often to help balance the tractor on these occasions by sitting above the front wheels, thus countering the weight of the engine. But if I were not there Geoffrey would still pursue his self-appointed task; and then I would catch him by surprise, the noise of the engine hiding my arrival, and I would find him reaching the top of a meadow, clutching the steering wheel, and the front wheels of the tractor an inch or so free of the ground they were travelling over. Daylight between wheels and soil. Plough still in its furrow. A sight which suggested that at any instant there could be a tragedy.

'Geoffrey!' I would shout above the rumble of the diesel, 'don't you realise the risk you're taking?'

He did not want to realise. He was having fun out of the challenge he was creating; he was covering with a tractor the same kind of ground which he used to dig with a shovel, so had he not got something to prove? He was securing a victory over tradition. He would have something to boast about.

'You should have seen me,' he yelled back at me, grinning, 'when I was ploughing that piece above the obs where the badgers are.'

I had already observed the result. He had ploughed a previously unproductive bracken-covered piece of land, part of which was a badgers' playground. He had done it when I was out for the day, and it was so steep that I would have thought twice before driving the Land Rover over it. It was a neat example of ploughing. But Geoffrey had driven the tractor and plough across the hill, as if he were inviting it to upset; and the last furrow was within a couple of feet of a bank which dropped three feet to the meadow where the obs bloomed in the spring, the miniature King Alfred daffodils with an ugly name, yet so exquisite to look at.

'I'll have to get Emily to talk to you,' I said, Emily being his fiancée, 'perhaps she'll make you see sense.'

It is my weakness that I prefer to carry someone with me instead of imposing my wishes. I find it easier to appeal rather than to order. And if you have a concern

77

like ours, so small and intimate, it is more essential than ever to have a spirit of cooperation. In my anxiety to achieve this cooperation I find I usually expect too much. I so desire to skirt the prospect of a mood on the part of someone I am employing, that I fall into the trap of failing to give clear orders. I prefer to rely on a kind of telepathy. I state the position as I see it, then expect the individual concerned to react in the same way, wishfully and foolishly thinking that my tedious process of thought has been shared by the other. I forget that I was alone when I assessed the future; that I alone endure the strains of raising finance, of carrying the burden of a crop disaster, of hoping to see daylight in another year. I should not expect the wage-earner to feel and think as I do.

Geoffrey, for instance, used the tractor more as a sport, while for me it was a weapon in a campaign. It was a fine weapon, but within a year I knew that it alone would not solve our problems. I was forced to realise that, although we were now able to cultivate so much more of our land and thus increase the scope of our crops, prosperity did not follow. We were too dependent on the weather. We were unbalanced. We were also at the tail-end of an era and this we had yet to wake up to.

We had come to Minack when any amateur could make a living out of flowers and new potatoes in our part of Cornwall provided he had decent land and worked hard enough. The mildness of the winter and the earliness of the spring meant that West Cornwall followed the Scilly Isles with daffodils. There was a leapfrog of daffodil harvests that went on all the way up the country from the Scillies to Lincolnshire; and because the Scillies and the Land's End area were earliest we naturally had the best prices. In those days the Channel Islands did not grow the vast quantities they grow now. Nor were there pre-cooled bulbs housed in acres of greenhouses throughout the country, producing artificial daffodil harvests all through the period when we used to have the markets to ourselves.

So, too, with potatoes. The new potatoes dug from the cliffs along the edge of Mount's Bay were considered both as a delicacy and a necessity. The grind of carrying the seed down the steep paths to the meadows, the planting, the weeks of caring for the plants, the shovelling out of the crop, the wearisome climb back up the cliff with the harvest . . . all this effort was repaid with a fair price. In those days the harvests of other countries were not being shipped into the country at the same time. In our part of Cornwall one could risk the spite of the weather because one year's profit would cover another year's losses. Our laborious efforts faced no competition.

There were the other flowers, the violets, anemones, stocks, wallflowers, calendulas, forget-me-nots – all these could earn their living. Wages were low and so was the cost of transport; and there were no jets speeding flowers to Covent Garden from all parts of the world. The cities needed our flowers and were ready to pay for them.

Thus when Jeannie and I began our life at Minack our course appeared to be straightforward. We had to absorb the tradition of the area, and the best way to do so was to ferret out the old hands, seeking their advice and following it. In our innocence we thought this method would be foolproof. We had no clue that science and the cost of living were on the verge of destroying the old standards. We held the simple belief that we had only to master the technicalities of growing the crops which everyone else grew in the area, for us to earn a living. For the climate was an unshakeable ally. It would overcome our inexperience. All we had to do was to listen and learn and work.

We used, therefore, to hang on to the words of the old growers as attentively as we used to listen to prominent politicians at times of crisis. We would fuss over an old chap in a pub about the merits of wallflowers with the same zest as we once sat in the Savoy's Grill Bar hearing the confidential views of some editor.

'Mark my words,' the old chap would say, sipping his beer, 'wallflowers are a proper crop. Cheap seed, can treat 'em rough, quick to pick, and a shilling a bunch.'

This was the kind of remark we loved to hear. A high priest was talking. He was passing us on information as valuable as a bar of gold. We used to go back home to the cottage, take pencil and paper, and calculate; and the calculation used to make us dizzy with excitement. It was simple. If we grew several thousand wallflowers we really would not have to grow anything else.

And there was another line of talk which warmed our hearts. It happened whenever someone praised Minack and hinted at its golden future. I remember meeting a taciturn farmer who charmed me by describing the land around Minack as the best in the district. Such flattery coming from one who was noted for his lack of good humour impressed me greatly; and I hastened to ask him why he thought so and what he would grow in my place. He was recognised as a very good farmer and his family had lived in the district for generations.

His eyes lit up.

'Taties along those cliffs,' he said, his voice coming to life, 'have fetched ten shillings a pound . . . and princeps eight shillings a bunch!'

He had no cliffs on his farm. He had had no opportunity to share the exploitation of the war and post-war years. It had rankled ever since. It had so seared into his mind that the cliffs had become to him a golden mirage. He was envious of me. He jealously saw a glorious future for me as a grower of potatoes and a picker of princeps, the hedgerow daffodil the most common of all. Greed had pushed him to praise the land around Minack.

But this I did not realise at the time. Nor did I appreciate that many of the others who made us happy by their remarks were only reflecting frustration. We had the chance which they wished for themselves, although in fact the value of the chance was wildly inflated. Their envy sprang from an extinct El Dorado. A memory which had no relation to the present or the future.

The aura of their attention, however, had its effect on Jeannie and me. It blinded us. We never for an instant saw that progress would be our danger and there would come a time when the system of our kind of market garden would have to change. The cliffs, we thought, were immune. The softness of West Cornwall everlasting. The only challenge that had to be met lay in ourselves. We had to emulate the peasant. We had to bring ourselves so close to the earth that we knew by instinct how to tend our crops. This, and patience and an endless capacity to accept hard labour were all we required to achieve prosperity at Minack.

Then, as the years passed, we began to realise that this formula did not measure up to its simplicity. The realisation came slowly, like the drip of water on a stone. We had found our perfect environment but we were losing the material battle. We had considered ourselves isolated from the penalties of progress. We had freed ourselves from the entanglements of conformism. No electricity, no telephone, no television. We were peasants. We were spared the impact of an industrial society. We had no need to look over our shoulders, catching sight of those who wished for our jobs. We were independent. Hard labour our pleasure. And yet, like a creeping paralysis, we were being embraced again by the fears we had left behind.

What ought we to do? It was in April that I most often used to pose this question. April was our month of assessment. We were between harvests. It was the month in which we measured the results of the flower season just ended and began preparing for the next. One winter merged with another, meadows of discarded plants alongside others of rich, bare soil, awaiting seeds.

Where once bloomed the daffodils were carpets of green foliage. Here and there were flickers of yellow, heads which were damaged or had come too late for market. There was desolation under the April sky; the daffodils had erupted in their glory, smiled their loveliness in a thousand, thousand homes, and were now forgotten. I would wander amidst the green waste remembering that the Magnificence had had a poor year or the King Alfreds a good one, or that by some curious chance the once-despised California had brought us the most money.

I would stare at the winter-flowering wallflowers, shorn of their primrose and stained orange and deep red blooms, sticking up from the ground like cabbage stalks. I would remember the seeds last April, the weeding, the transplanting in June, the weeding again, the wonderful moment in November when enough stems were plucked from the plants for the first box to be sent on the flower train from Penzance. A year of caressing, and battering gales, and sweet scents, and heavy baskets lugged to the packing shed; and now they awaited obliteration from the rotovator and the plough.

Sporadic flowers peered from the beds of anemones, stocks and violets; and, maddeningly, the beds of calendula were a riot of orange. I would look at them thinking of the frost which crushed their buds into pulp, delaying them for weeks until, the season ended, they were no longer wanted. The violet plants, plump green cushions, were reaching to each other across the rows, perfume from the leaves touching the air; row upon row of them ready for dismemberment, a dozen runners from each, to be pushed into the ground in May, to fatten in the summer, to bloom again in the autumn. It was always thus in April; we ended and we began.

What ought we to do? I do not make wise decisions when I try to be logical. My arguments, on either side of the problem involved, cancel each other out with such effect that I am left hanging in midair; and I do nothing. I like, therefore, to act out of emotion. I find that what successes I have had in my life have been born out of flashes of insight, the seizure of an opportunity which would have died a sudden death had I stopped to reason. And I have usually found that a most inconsequential event promotes the opportunity I need.

One April afternoon a few months after the tractor had been bought, Jeannie and I had gone into the packing shed with the idea of cleaning it up. The odd dried daffodil stalk lay on the floor in the corner, a few withered leaves of wallflowers under the table, cardboard boxes, bottoms and tops, were strewn on a shelf, address labels and contents labels were higgledy-piggledy on the windowsill like a spilt pack of cards. Jam jars, galvanised flower pails, some still undrained; and at random on shelves and table were the clippers which trimmed the daffodil stems, a much thumbed invoice book, rubber bands small enough for the violets and big enough for the wallflowers, a stapling machine to fix the labels, a half-used ream of white paper, and flower sticks with their metal sharp ends which secure the bunches in the boxes after they have been packed. We began to put order into this chaos when Geoffrey suddenly appeared at the door.

'What's up, Geoffrey?'

He looked at me shamefaced, a smile trying to hover. 'Tractor's upset.'

I had been expecting this to happen for so long that at first I accepted his news as calmly as if he had been reporting that his shovel had broken. Then I had wonderment and thankfulness that he was unhurt. It was incredible.

It had happened in our big field which slopes unevenly down to the top of the cliff and which is locally known as the cemetery field . . . so called because from time immemorial the old cattle and horses used to be buried at the bottom where the hedge crests the cliff. He had been charging across it when a rear wheel hit a rock, he was flung out, and the tractor somersaulted down the hill and came to rest with its wheels in the air.

I could not, of course, refrain from pointing out to him the number of times I had warned him what would happen if he continued to drive so fast; but I could not be angry. For one thing he was so ashamed, for another, the tractor had miraculously suffered only superficial damage. Indeed, having inspected it and, with Geoffrey, pushed it back on to its wheels, I had a curious feeling of elation. A magic had saved us from tragedy. I had such a sense of happiness and gratitude that I wanted to burst into song. It was in this mood I returned to the cottage and found a stranger awaiting me.

He was a salesman of greenhouses. He seemed surprised by the enthusiasm with which I greeted him. He was accustomed to make the patter of sales talk, but here was I bubbling with excitement.

I suddenly knew what we had to do. One greenhouse was not enough. We had to have more. And I was not going to listen to the logic that we could not afford them.

6

I launched my grandiose plan before I had time for second thoughts. It was flamboyant. It had no relation to our financial resources but it projected an image of such likely security that the cost could look after itself.

I ordered two mobile greenhouses each seventy feet long and eighteen feet wide, and provisionally ordered two more.

This fling at the fates so intoxicated our imaginations that we drew up a blueprint for the coming year so vast in its scope that if it came off our material problems would be solved for ever. It was also sensible. We were not allowing our enthusiasm to interfere with our judgement. And yet, in retrospect I wonder if our gesture was not prompted by an emotion similar to that of a losing boxer in the closing rounds of a fight . . . fists flying in a desperate bid for a win. We had lost patience with caution. It was time to take a gamble.

We planned a two-pronged attack, outdoors and under cover. We would, for instance, make use of every piece of land we had, and because of the tractor there would be no delay in preparing it. We would grow all the usual flowers but on a far bigger scale. A quarter of an acre of calendula, an acre of anemones, three quarters of an acre of wallflowers, thousands of violets, tons of daffodils, beds and beds of winter-flowering stock, and a mass of Blue Bird forget-me-nots.

The physical problem of planting all these was, of course, formidable. But by the end of the summer the land was filled with our potential income; and most important of all, the two mobile greenhouses were erected. These were our pride.

They looked like miniature glass aircraft hangars on wheels, small wheels which rested on rails that enabled them, in our particular case, to be moved over two sites; and this meant we were able to grow two crops at the same time, one already covered, one waiting to be covered.

They appeared perilously exposed to the weather. They stood in the field bordering the lane and although to the west they had the protection of the wood, they were certain to be hit by the northerly and easterly and the terrible fierceness of the southerly. I do not believe I would have ordered them if I had thought twice, if I had not been flushed by the mood of abandon which struck me after the tractor overturned. I would have been too frightened. I would have seen disaster ahead. The gales were waiting. The hands of the wind would find the gaps by the wheels and lift them up. How could I expect such a greenhouse to stand up to a fury which could obliterate an outside crop in a night? After all, even our hundred-foot greenhouse, firmly based on foundations, shivered when the gales blew.

We were, however, so stimulated by the pattern that

lay ahead that we were able to dispense with such antici-
patory fears. We at last were upsetting the much-used
curriculum of growing potatoes. For year after year we
had grown potatoes and the luck was always against us.
Gales had blasted them, droughts had hit them, frosts
had turned them into pulp, gluts had ruined the price.
There never was a year when Jeannie and I lolled in the
pleasure of a great success. The early potato harvest
from the cliffs was economically dead. We had been
trying to live on a dying tradition.

Instead we would now become big tomato growers.
The tedious labour of the cliffs would be replaced by
the more gentle task of tending the tomato plants in the
greenhouses. We had already proved we had a market
on the doorstep and so there was no expense of transport. Our summer income seemed assured.

We then had to decide what flowers we should grow
in the greenhouses during the winter; and we received
the usual bewildering assortment of advice. Every bulb
and flower in the catalogue was deemed suitable for our
attention; and we pored over the lists, paper and pencil
in hand, calculating possible financial returns based on
the figures of the previous year's market reports.

Jeannie was very earnest. She drew diagrams, for
instance, of pre-cooled daffodil bulbs represented by dots,
hundreds of little dots representing the bulbs in a bed,
then a blank space for a path, and more hundreds of little dots. And she finally added them all up and divided by
twelve, and announced how many bunches there would
be to pick. There were simpler ways of calculating, but
Jeannie obstinately preferred this visual method.

At last we decided that in one of the mobiles we would have a slow-moving harvest, forget-me-nots that would bring us an income January onwards; and in the other we would have a quick, all in one week, harvest of Wedgewood iris, which would rush into readiness at the end of March. And in the big static house we would grow the Giant Pacific polyanthus.

Thus out plans were laid for the distant spring and the summer to follow. The money was there in the growing crops, but meanwhile we had to live. We also had to cope with the vast amount of work without employing extra labour, extra labour which was needed, but which we could not afford. In time, if all went well and the crops mastered the winter, we would have to find someone to help with the harvests. It would be pleasant to do so. The money would be coming in so that it would not hurt paying out. The hurt was now during the long wait.

There was a struggle every week to pay Geoffrey's and Jane's wages. Saturday morning would arrive and I would count the notes and hand them over; and then I would return to Jeannie and say that I envied them as wage-earners. Jeannie and I had aimed at the splendours of individualism without computing what such freedom demands. Personal freedom is a word, not a fact. Personal freedom creates its own chains. We were expanding, but the expansion had burdened us with more commitments; expansion was inescapable if we were to keep on Geoffrey and Jane and lift our own lives above those of peasants. We had to spend in order to remain free.

But the wonder of our life was that we never wished

to shift its base. There in the lonely cottage where the sea murmured through the windows, we had the exquisite knowledge that if the map of the world had been open to us and we could go where we chose, money no object, we would have lived nowhere else. We were the lucky ones. We had an environment which cushioned us against the worries which burrow and sap confidence. We were living the life of our choice and Minack was our armour. We were not looking out at the horizon like others, searching for a life that is beyond reach. We did not have to say we would find happiness if we did this or did that, having to brighten the greyness of the passing years by praying that one day a dream would be fulfilled. We had our dream around us; and if there were times when the conventional stresses of living jabbed at us, challenging the sincerity of our happiness, we could not for long remain depressed. For we only had the trouble in hand to face.

We had a particular crisis that summer which required all our resources to defeat. It was a prolonged crisis which went on for week after week. Every day we waited anxiously for the postman to come across the fields; and when the expected letter arrived I would have to spend hours writing convincing answers to the questions the letter contained. I replied to a score of such letters that summer; and when in the end the crisis was over, when on a glorious August morning a letter arrived to tell us we could have a measure of financial help until the promised harvest came next spring, I rushed out to Geoffrey and Jane to give them the good news.

This gesture was, of course, only a reflex of my own

relief. As each week we struggled to pay their wages, I had identified them in my mind as part of our struggle. This is what happens in a small business. I, for instance, faced with my anxiety to pay the wages, had become so consumed with my efforts to do so, that I found myself believing that Geoffrey and Jane had shared my anxiety. Hence, now that Jeannie and I had won a reprieve, I had an irresistible desire that they should share our delight. It was an indulgence. It was also a thankfulness that now I would be able to look at them on a Saturday morning without grudging the wage they deserved.

First I saw Geoffrey, who was digging a ditch in the wood, and when I shouted to him that everything was now all right, he paused for a moment resting on his shovel. Geoffrey has a kind face. He has blue eyes. He is very strong, and he is perhaps the best handyman I have ever known. He could be a plumber or a mason, and memories of his art remain tangible at Minack to this day. He looked at me, half smiling, and he obviously could not understand what it was I was so excited about. I passed on to Jane.

She was thinning lettuce plants in the stable meadow. As usual she was barefooted, looking like some Continental peasant child, uncomplicated, utterly free, the wonderful fair hair touching her shoulders.

'Jane!' I shouted, 'we're all right!'

It was such conceit on my part that I could believe she should understand my enthusiasm. Why did I expect so? She was only sixteen and a half. And yet she had that kind of enthusiasm which flared such sincerity that both Jeannie and I felt its benefit. Jane, both Jeannie and I felt, was part of us. And Jeannie and Jane talked to each other as if there were no difference in their ages. For both, life was a gay excitement; and for me who saw them together, it was wondrous to see two different generations together as if passing time did not exist.

'Jane! Isn't it wonderful?'

Her response to good news, even if she did not know its significance, was usually effervescent. If I had a letter containing some pleasant information and I told her, I could rely on her to react happily despite the fact that I had not given her the details of its contents. She was by nature an enthusiast. She would, for instance, appear as pleased as we were when we received news that prices for our flowers had gone up. It was part of the fun to tell her. She never failed to add to it.

And yet on this particular day she was disappointing me. She did not look me in the face, and to my surprise there was no smile to show she was glad. She stared at the ground, scratching the soil with the hoe within an inch or two of her bare feet. Of course she did not know the extent of the tremendous relief in my mind, and so I was plainly expecting too much from her. But always before there had been the telepathy conveying the mood of our excitement. It was obviously not working on this occasion.

Suddenly she looked up, but instead of meeting my eyes she looked to one side. Something was wrong. Whenever Jane was confused her cheeks became like red berries and her eyes wandered in every direction except straight in front of her.

'I've been meaning to tell you, Mr Tangye,' and in

a flash I knew my high excitement was about to disappear, 'I'm leaving.'

I have sensed sometimes that someone who is working for me is thinking of going. There is a look about them, a slight casualness, a confidence towards me that they did not previously display. I am aware they are saying to themselves: 'I've been here long enough. It's time to move on.' It's a dying relationship between us, a product of ennui, the job has become dulled by the routine. I am therefore prepared.

But I was not by Jane.

'Say that again.' It was I who had now become flushed. I was thinking purely of myself. The thrill of overcoming our problem, the moment of celebration, was to be dissipated. Instead of relaxing for the first day in weeks, the weariness of the burden we had carried clear of our shoulders, here quickly was another to take its place.

'You see, Mr Tangye,' she said, and she had suddenly become animated, a bubbling enthusiasm which certainly had nothing to do with Minack, 'Mum and I are going to Turkey.'

This was a surprise.

'Yes,' she said, and because I was showing interest her confidence was returning, 'We're going in a van with two friends, and camping all the way, and when we get to Turkey we're going to live near Ankara, and grow our own vegetables, and spend our time digging for buried treasure.'

The programme was rushed out breathlessly and I would have laughed had it not been Jane who had spoken. True she used to have wild enthusiasms, but she was also so sensible. I respected her opinions. If she told me that a certain section of our work could be improved this way or that, I would generally have reason to agree with her. She thought out her work. She had a sense of responsibility. Had we gone away at any time and left her in charge I would never have worried. She was deliciously reliable.

'I really don't see how you can live on vegetables,' I said, and there was a note of condescension in my voice, 'after all, they take time to grow and what do you do in the meantime?'

My condescension was not as real as it sounded. I had a certain understanding for such a crazy idea. I had had so many myself which had been laughed at by outsiders. I was once fired as a columnist of a daily newspaper on a Wednesday, only to announce on the Thursday that I had resigned in order to go round the world. My friends at the time thought it was a complicated alibi to explain my dismissal. I knew better. I had an excuse to force myself into doing what I had always wanted to do.

Jane's mind would always range widely. She could not always thin lettuces or pinch out tomatoes or enjoy the leisurely pleasure of a peasant girl. She was too intelligent ever to be cushioned against conflict. And her mother felt the same; she was alert to the knowledge that Jane looked for adventure however small might be its canvas. Why not give her a chance for a real adventure?

'Oh, we've planned how to live in the meantime.'

She was returning my condescension in a way I had learned to associate with her. When in doubt she was most superior. She set out to swipe her opponent out of the arena by the sheer force of her character. She *knew*. The opponent didn't.

'I won't be going immediately,' she said encouragingly, 'but I wanted you to know in good time. I'm awfully sorry . . .'

I returned to the cottage and told Jeannie the news. At first she laughed at my solemn face and said the whole idea was absurd and that it would never materialise.

'You know Jane!'

But when I described the way Jane had told me, how it seemed to be different from her other enthusiasms that had melted away, she began to share my concern. After all Jane had given in her notice. That was final enough; and she had too cool an intellect to do that unless she and her mother had made their final decision. And as we discussed it, both Jeannie and I became vexed. The day's pleasure was being sidetracked. Instead of celebrating our personal achievement, we were talking about Jane. Who should we get to take her place? Did we want a girl or should we have a boy to help Geoffrey? The tedious worries of an employer, bitty and sterile. Round and round the same subject and going nowhere. She won't leave, she will. Jane, Jane, Jane . . .

Then we asked ourselves why we were so concerned whether Jane stayed or left. She was certainly thorough but she had not the knowledge to make her indispensable. We could easily find someone to take her place. So why waste time talking about her?

It was her attitude to life that we wanted to keep. Young as she was, she was in tune with us. An essence of happiness is to wake up in the morning and look forward to seeing the people with whom you are going to work. If you are at ease with them, if they are friends and not robots, if they do not irritate you, if they are not envious, then another dimension enters your life. Time does not drag. Evenings are not wasted worrying about the mishaps of the day. And if you are small employers the weight of responsibility is lightened, the enthusiasm of cooperation becoming as important as the technical ability to do the job.

There was the basic fact that Jane possessed the same wild love for the coast along which we lived as we did ourselves. It is no ordinary coast. The stretch where Minack lies and where Jane's cottage still stands gaunt, staring out at the ocean, is not the kind of country which appeals to the conformist. The splendour of the cliffs does not lead to beaches where people can crowd together, transistors beside them.

The cliffs fall to rocks black and grey where the sea ceaselessly churns, splashing its foam, clutching a rock then releasing it, smothering it suddenly in bad temper, caressing it, slapping it as if in play, sometimes kind with the sun shining on the white ribbon of a wave, a laughing sea throwing spray like confetti, sometimes grey and sullen, then suddenly again a sea of ungovernable fury lashing the cliffs; enraged that for ever and for ever the cliffs look down.

And among the rocks are the pools; some that tempt yet are vicious, beckoning innocently then in a flash a cauldron of currents, pools that are shallow so that the minnow fish ripple the surface as they dash from view, pools so deep that the seaweed looks like a forest far below, inaccessible pools, pools which hide from everyone except those who belong to them.

High above, the little meadows dodge the boulders, and where the land is too rough for cultivation the bracken, the hawthorn, the brambles, the gorse which sparks its yellow the year round, reign supreme. This is no place for interlopers. The walkers, tamed by pavements, faced by the struggling undergrowth, turn back or become angry, their standardised minds piqued that they have to trace a way through; and it is left to the few, the odd man or woman, to marvel that there is a corner of England still free from the dead hand of the busybody.

The badgers show the way. Their paths criss-cross, twist, turn, pound the soil flat, a foot wide, high roads of centuries, and when the bracken greens or coppers the land, the way is still there, underneath, so that if you have a feel for the countryside the undergrowth does not halt you. The badgers lead you. As you walk, feet firm and safe, you part the bracken to either side and after you have passed, it folds back again, leaving no sign of your passage.

Here, on our stretch of the coast, man has not yet brought his conceit. It is as it always has been. Gulls sweeping on their way, a buzzard sailing in the sky, foxes safe from the Hunt, birds arriving tired after a long journey, others ready to leave, swallows, white-throats, chiffchaffs, fieldfare, snipe, the long list which we welcome and to which we say goodbye. Our stretch of the cliff has a savagery that frightens the faint-hearted.

'Why isn't there a decent path cut out along the cliff top? Absolutely disgraceful.'

'All right in the summer, I suppose?'

'I wouldn't live here if it was given me.'

'How wonderful if uranium was discovered!'

'There's going to be a coastal path. You can't escape it, you know!'

'This is marvellous. An August day in Cornwall and no one to be seen.'

There they are, the philistines and the individual they would like to destroy. Mass enjoyment, mass organised walks, mass anything if it can score a victory over the sensitive; thus the philistines, barren of feeling, plod their dreary way, earnest, dull, conscientious, honest, misguided – I pity them. So did Jane. But Jane, like ourselves, was infuriated by their conceit.

Every day of our lives was spent in unison with this coast, the rage of the gales, salt smearing our faces as we walked, east winds, south winds, calm summer early mornings, the first cubs, a badger in the moonlight, wild violets, the glory of the first daffodil, the blustering madness of making a living on land that faced the roar of the ages. These were the passages of our year. Glorious, hurting, awakening us to the splendour of living. But the philistines. They nose. They want to disturb. Yet they are blind to beauty. They glance at our coast as they rush by. They want to see a path on the map. That is their object. Everything must conform. No time to pause. Hurry, hurry, hurry . . . we have another two miles to go.

Once there was an uncommunicative young man who spent a month on behalf of some Ministry, mysteriously hammering on the rocks of our cliff, making a map and taking samples from the results of his hammering. His presence immediately alerted us to the possible dangers of his activity. Was he looking for uranium? Or tin? Or some other metal vital for industrial progress?

And only a few weeks afterwards, on a hot June day while we were digging potatoes, an aeroplane had droned to and fro all the day long over our heads, towing a box-like contraption several plane lengths behind. It angered us. And while Geoffrey and I plunged our shovels up the rows, and Jeannie and Jane knelt picking up the potatoes and putting them in the baskets, our conversation buzzed over the possible threat the box might represent. It also, of course, provided a diversion from our monotonous task. Jane seized my shovel, at one stage, stood in the middle of a meadow and with the mock fury of a native who had seen a white man for the first time, pretended to hurtle the shovel at the plane like a spear.

Her response, however, to the young man with the hammer had been mischievous. He was shy and desperately earnest and although both Jane and ourselves tried to get him into conversation as he went to and fro his rocks every day, all we were able to extract from him was a 'Good morning' and a 'Good evening'.

It was Easter and on the Sunday the young man arrived to perform his hammering on some lonely rock beneath the cliffs. It was beneath Jane's section of the cliff and before climbing below, he had dumped his haversack in a meadow that sloped steeply from Jane's cottage. He was, however, unaware that he had dumped it exactly in the middle of the area in which a regular Easter game was about to be played; for in Jane's family there was a tradition to hide each other's Easter presents outside in a chosen area of ground. In the garden, or, as on this occasion, somewhere in the meadows in front of the cottage. Jane, her mother and young Jeremy played their game, and then Jane decided to play another.

She took two small chocolate eggs wrapped in silver paper, stole down to the haversack and placed them neatly so that the young man would see them as soon as he returned from his duties. Later that day she saw him clamber up the cliff and arrive at his haversack; then she waited for his reaction. None. He hesitated for a moment, then strapped up the haversack and hoisted it on his back, and marched off. But what delighted Jane was that he kept the Easter eggs, he made no gesture of throwing them away. And so, because she was fanciful and because next day he made no mention of his find, she came to a happy conclusion. The young man had believed a pixie had put them there.

Jane had no fear of climbing the cliffs and some-times I called her foolhardy. There was one section the marine commandos used to use for climbing practice. They came in their boats from Newlyn, then nosed inshore, and one by one they sprang on a sea-lashed rock; or they fell in the water. I have seen a dozen in the sea swimming in their life-jackets.

Their attempts would be watched by Jane who, after they had gone, would clamber to the spot they had chosen and begin to climb herself. She had the good sense not to go very far but she felt forced to make the attempt; it was a challenge and she was always looking for a challenge.

Heaven knows how she ever reached her secret bathing pool, which could not be seen from anywhere above; and then climbed back afterwards. Jeremy, her brother, never dared do it, and he was adventurous enough. It lay in a zone below the cottage, first a steep grass slope, then a sheer drop of a hundred feet, except for a narrow grassy ledge which fell like an almost perpendicular toboggan run on one side.

I do not know how anyone could stay on the ledge without slithering to the rocks at high speed unless there was a rope to hold. Jane never had a rope. And she thought so lightly of the risk, that on hot summer days she would rush back from Minack at lunchtime so that she could spend the greater part of her hour splashing in her pool and sunbathing beside it.

High above and eastwards towards Minack was the meadow she called her own. It was cradled in a cliff called Carn Silver, fifty feet above the sea and facing south to the Wolf. She reached it by a tortuous path that could never have been found by a stranger, and that, of course, was part of her fun. It was her own meadow and, she once told me, it seemed to welcome her as if it were alive, as if it were an animal. It was edged by man-placed stones, but it had been neglected for scores of years, and so it was perhaps possible that the spirits were glad Jane had become their chatelaine. She suited them. Her ways belonged to them.

It was here in this meadow of about thirty feet

square that she carried out her market garden activities. They were not, of course, of the scope which merited the name market garden, but she had a game which she enjoyed and this was to pretend that it was indeed a market garden. Hence she used to write to various horticultural suppliers heading her notepaper after the name by which the three cottages were known. The Pentewan Nurseries, she called herself and her meadow.

She liked digging the meadow by moonlight. I wonder what the badgers and foxes said to themselves as this mid-twentieth-century teenager, long fair hair over her shoulders, sturdy, utterly content, jabbed the spade into the turf; for at first it was hard going, the ground had to be turned and the result waited upon, before it became soil. There she was, poised above the restless sea, the moonlight giving the Carn behind her its name, watched by the wild, sensed by the spirits, echoing the ageless effort of the peasant.

'How did you get on?' I would ask her next day.

'I think I'll finish it in another two nights.' Her voice, as always, piped. Voices that are high can irritate. They can provide the effect of a false note. One feels sometimes that the person behind such a voice is shallow and that their behaviour is designed for effect. Jane pretended, she wrapped herself in illusions, but hers was always a true part in a glorious game.

In due course Pentewan Nurseries began to have callers or, to be exact, callers tried to find out where to call. A representative of a famous seed establishment, another on behalf of a world-renowned fertiliser company, another who had special lightweight flower boxes to sell, another who had a rotovator to demonstrate, these people wandered the district looking for Jane's meadow.

On one occasion a Dutchman who had come to see me at Minack told me his next call was at Pentewan Nurseries and solemnly asked me to direct him. We have a number of Dutchmen who visit us during the year selling bulbs. They are an earnest, persistent lot. They have a silver-tongued patter which is persuasive and it was particularly persuasive in the years after the war when daffodil prices were high.

The farmers, envious of their horticultural neighbours, set out to plant bulbs as if they were turnips. They were also fascinated, since many of them had never left their own parishes, by the charming broken accent of the Dutchmen. It was a hint of the great world beyond, of naughty Europe, of sophistication they only read about. The Dutchmen played upon this weakness with such effect that West Cornwall was swamped with bulbs, and where cattle should peacefully have grazed, there were acres of daffodils. The honeymoon did not last very long. The farmers defeated themselves. They bought so many bulbs that they were incapable of looking after the daffodils. They had neither the time to grade and pack to professional standards, nor the wish to do so. They were only interested in the cream of the market and a quick return; and so when prices began to fall and daffodils were no longer easy money, they gave them up. And the charming Dutchmen had to be glib elsewhere.

They came often down the lane to Minack, in small cars with a left-hand drive, so easily recognisable that if one of us saw a flashing glimpse of the car through a gap far up the lane we would shout: 'Look out, a Dutchman's coming!'

We were a little malicious towards them. Jane, in particular, liked to tease them, although they had no notion that the teasing was in progress. She hatched a plot, for instance, to deal with those Dutchmen to whom I owed money.

It was easy to owe them money because part of their salesmanship was to offer credit until the flowers were in bloom. The fact that a glut had occurred, the prices had been low, and we had made a loss on the deal did not, of course, matter. The bulbs had proved their virility. And inevitably in the spring the Dutchmen would be coming down the lane to collect their cheque.

It was for this reason that Jane devised a series of compost heaps, each of which bore the name of a creditor. She got the idea from a story Jeannie told her from a thriller she had read. A gentleman, famed for his prize vegetables, had murdered his wife and buried her under the compost heap which was the envy of his neighbours. The story titilated Jane.

Her theory was that anyone who was so bold as to come to lonely Minack asking for money should be attacked, then buried in the compost heap allocated to him. Hence, when one of these people arrived, I would catch sight of her in the background making elaborate, fanciful signs denoting the method of his disposal. Sometimes, as I solemnly talked, I would see her aiming at the back of a creditor as if she possessed a bow and arrow, and the arrow was about to fly. I have also seen her, when looking over the shoulder of my visitor, performing bloodcurdling gestures with a knife; the creditor's throat was being symbolically cut.

On one occasion there was an especially tough creditor, a man so dominated by his mission that he failed to praise the glory of the coastline. Such a failure vexed Jane as much as it did ourselves. We judged people by the degree of enthusiasm they displayed for our coast. Those who said how awful it must be in winter, as if the isolation could only be tolerated in summer, were placed by Jane and ourselves at the bottom of the dustbin. This particular creditor seemed to think that Minack was an appalling place in which to live a twentieth-century pattern, winter and summer.

Jeannie, nevertheless, because it was teatime, was prepared to offer him a cup of tea. The creditor and I were on a white seat outside the cottage and I saw Jeannie, as I sat there, hand Jane a cup, then Jane disappeared for a moment.

When she appeared again she came up to the gentleman with a low bow and handed him his cup. There was a glint in her eye.

'Thank you very much,' said the man.

'I *hope* you'll enjoy it,' said Jane.

She had, in her fanciful fashion, allocated him his compost and, equally fancifully, had contrived a method of getting him there. It consisted of a potion, now emptied into the cup, of stewed stinging nettles, chickweed and heliotrope. She had planned the potion as soon as I told her, a few days before, that this particular gentleman was coming to visit me. He was very polite. He drank his tea without complaint. And, of

105

course, he does not know to this day that in theory he is part of a compost.

After this episode we called Jane a witch. 'Cast a spell, Jane,' we would say whenever there was something we particularly desired.

But here was a Dutchman asking me the whereabouts of Pentewan Nurseries; and obviously I could not betray Jane by describing it as a meadow thirty feet square poised on an inaccessible cliff. It was my duty to support her. The matter had to be treated seriously. So I said:

'The proprietor of Pentewan Nurseries *helps* here. I'll introduce you.'

My introduction was enough to speed Jane's idea of fun to such an extent that the Dutchman, innocent, was talking in terms of tons of bulbs for Pentewan Nurseries. I felt, as I listened, that he was aware that something might be wrong, but the prospect of his commission confused him. This was an opportunity. A new customer. And the girl was obviously knowledgeable.

It is an art to know at what moment to end a joke, and Jane never persevered too long. She disengaged quietly. She did not close the session of joking with a guffaw, forcing her victim into blustering embarrassment. She slid out of the joke. She left a question mark in the victim's mind. And the Dutchman departed, a suspicion of a smile on his face, wondering whether she would indeed write to him about the order she promised to consider.

So was she joking about going to Turkey? Was it a whim or a jest to say that she was leaving us? Perhaps the mood we were in had deprived Jeannie and me of a sense of humour. We had no laughter to spare. We had been drained by the weary struggle for survival, our senses had been deadened by the pitiless monotony of pretence; the pretence to be prosperous, the pretence to be gay, the pretence to have hope when none seemed to exist. Far from the cities, esconced in the home of our dreams, we could not escape the twentieth-century malady. The sordid routine pursued us. And now on the day that we had momentarily rejoiced in a reprieve, here was Jane telling us she was going.

'It's no use worrying about it any more,' said Jeannie, 'it's just a pity she didn't choose another day to tell us.'

. Weeks passed and nothing happened. The winter came and still the trek to Turkey was never mentioned. Then one windy, rainy November afternoon, Jeannie broached the question again at a moment when Jane had lugged a couple of baskets of wallflowers into the packing shed.

'Oh, Jane,' she said casually, 'what's happened to your Turkey trip?'

Jane heaped a pile of the wallflowers on to the table and started to strip off the leaves. She still wore her oil-skin. It was huge, black, and three times too big for her; and her sou'wester, also black, buried her head so that all you could see was a nose and a few strands of fair hair.

'We've decided not to go just yet,' she said. A firm little voice, a note of slight irritation in it that comes when one is asked about a plan which has miscarried.

'Not *yet*, at any rate,' she added.

The answer was all that Jeannie required. She knew her Jane.

The Turkey visit had been permanently postponed.

7

The spring came early the following year. In February there were gentle west winds, balmy days which sent the larks into the sky to sing a month before their time. The green woodpecker in the elms below the cottage clung to the bark tapping his note of joy, unperturbed that the splendour of his crimson crown among the bare branches was there for all to see. The sunshine was his safety.

There was a rush of wings in Minack woods. Exultant songs from the willows, blackbirds courting, and thrushes rivalling them with glorious notes. Harsh warbles from the chaffinches, and the trills of the wrens, fluffing their tiny bodies, then bellowing their happiness. Magpies coarsely cried. The two ravens from the cliff flew overhead coughing their comments on what they could see below. Robins were careless in hiding their nests, no time for danger, for spring was here. Owls hooted in the daylight. The wintering flocks of starlings gathered in the sky like black confetti, wondering whether to leave. Too soon for the chiffchaffs or the warblers or the whitethroats. They did not know we had an early spring. Minack woods still belonged to those who lived there.

The sea rippled in innocence, and when the *Scillonian* sailed by to and from the Islands we could hear in the cottage the pounding of her engines; for the wind and the surf were silent. Fishermen were tempted to drop their lobster pots, and one of them every day had a string across our tiny bay. There were others feathering for mackerel. Cockleshell white boats with men in yellow oilskins, engines chattering until the moment came to switch off and to drift with the tide. Gulls aimlessly dotted the water, like lazy holidaymakers. Cormorants on the edge of rocks held out their wings to dry like huge, motionless bats. The first primroses clustered on the cliff's edge and the white blooms of the blackthorn spattered the wasteland above. A beautiful spring, if only the task was to be part of it; but to us it held a threat. There was danger in the lovely days. There was menace in the soft breezes and warm nights. For our livelihood depended on cold. We required brisk weather and frosts up-a-long. How could we sell our flowers if flowers from everywhere were flooding the markets?

This was our first spring at Minack without Monty. He had died the previous May and lay buried beside the little stream that crossed the lane at the entrance to Minack, and which was for ever to be known as Monty's Leap. His shadow seemed always to be with us. And although when one loses a loved one it is necessary to be practical and not to mope or to be indulgently sentimental, we yearned for the soft fur curled at the bottom of our bed at night, the sudden purrs, the wonderful comfort of his greetings on our returns, the splendour of his person – the colour of autumn bracken – poised ready to pounce on a mouse rustling in the grass.

He had been part of our lives for so long. He had been a friend in the sense that he had always been there to cope with our disappointments, ready to be picked up and hugged or to bring calm with a game or to soothe by sitting on my lap and being gently stroked. He had been an anchor in our life. He was only a cat, but he had shared the years; and thus he would always be part of us.

I said to him on his last day that I would never have another cat. I felt, in saying this, that I was in some strange way repaying his love. I was giving him his identity. I was proving to him that he was not to me just one of a breed who could be replaced, like replacing a broken cup with one of the same pattern. He was Monty, and there would never be another. It would be no use some well-meaning person arriving at the door with a kitten, curbing grief by offering a substitute. I was telling him that I would always be loyal to him. The only cat I had ever known.

And then I made a remark that in retrospect was to prove so extraordinary. I found myself saying that I would make one exception . . . if a black cat whose previous home could never be discovered came crying to the door of the cottage in a storm. I was so astonished by my own words that I went and told Jeannie. I was ashamed by what I had said. At the very moment I was trying to prove my devotion, I had hedged. I had not meant what I had been saying to Monty. My emotion had deceived me and my subconscious had come out with the truth. I would, in fact, accept a successor. True, I was able to console myself by realising I had made an apparently impossible condition.

And now it was February, a wonderful summer-like February, nine months after he died, and there had been no sign of a black cat crying at the door. There had been no sign of any stray cat coming to Minack; and cats, except for Monty's memory, had been dismissed from my mind. We had other companions.

Old Hubert, the gull on the roof, continued to waddle along the ridge, staring down at us as we went about our business, sitting sometimes with feathers fluffed out at the top of the massive stone chimney, strutting in the garden, alighting on the cedarwood covering of the coal shed waiting for Jeannie to feed him.

He had been with us for six years, since that day we came up from the cliff aware that we had lost the rewards of our potato harvest to the weather, all our hopes gone, Tommy – who then worked for us – told to leave because we had no money for his wages, a moment of despair; and then we came up the path to the cottage and saw the gull on the roof.

He was to us the symbol we needed. The sight of him reassured us in the sense that at this moment of material defeat, the wild had suddenly accepted us as it had accepted the generations who had toiled at Minack before us. The gull had watched and now was prepared to trust. We had never attempted to lure him. We had never noticed him before. He was one of hundreds who flew every day in the sky above Minack, and he had chosen this moment of distress to adopt us. It was from that time that we felt we belonged to Minack, that we were no longer interlopers from the city imposing ourselves on the countryside, pretending in fact to be country people. We had passed the test. We were no longer looking on from the outside, armchair escapists who believe that dreams are real. We had been defeated, and there would be no soft way out for victory. We had joined the ghosts of Minack in the endless struggle against the seasons and, in doing so, we had embraced all the things they had seen and heard and done. We had become part of the ageless continuity of Minack; and the gull on the roof was its symbol.

And then there were Charlie the chaffinch and Tim the robin. Monty had treated these two with indifference, as indeed he did all birds. Yet both Charlie and Tim often gave him reasons to be justifiably irritated. Charlie, who was so gaily beautiful in the spring and summer and so drab in winter, used to hop around him as he lay somnolent in the garden as if he were playing a game of dare. And Tim used to tempt him by coming into the cottage and perching on the back of the chair upon which he was lying; then start to warble, softly, almost a gurgle.

We had not sought the friendship of Charlie or Tim. They each pushed their personalities into our lives. We had not set out to bribe them by the customary method of crumbs. It was just that we became gradually aware day after day, week after week, that a particular chaffinch and a particular robin took far more notice of us than any of the other birds in the neighbourhood.

Indeed their behaviour exactly suited our personal attitude to wildlife. It should come to man and not man to it. Some people like to try to conquer the natural instincts of a wild bird or animal, and then boast they have an unusual pet. True, it has required great patience on their part to score the victory but it always seems to me to be a hollow one. It makes me feel that vanity is the motive of the conquest, for it certainly cannot be of any benefit to the wild creature concerned. Its instincts will strive to be free again and, if it escapes, it will probably go to its doom by trusting other animals and men who are normally its enemy.

Jeannie was brought a fox cub once by a trapper who had found it in one of his snares. It was surprising that he had not killed it, for it was trapped in sheep country and foxes had been worrying the sheep in the neighbourhood; but it was so pitifully young, not a month old and perhaps caught on its first venture out from the earth, that he had not the heart to do so. He had made a special trip to Minack, for the snare had badly cut its right foot and it needed attention; and the trapper felt that Jeannie was the one to help.

He took it out of a basket and handed it to her and it immediately snuggled into her arms like a puppy. It looked so safe and harmless that I put out a finger to stroke it. I just touched it, and was nipped; but it never nipped Jeannie for the whole six weeks she looked after it. It was a male cub, and she called him Sammy.

For the first few days she kept him in a wire-covered box near the stove in the sitting room, teaching him to lap bread and milk from a saucer. Three or four times a day she bathed the foot and although it must have hurt him, he showed no resentment towards her. He obviously had complete trust.

We were about to plant tomatoes in our small greenhouse, a hundred and twenty plants direct into the soil. The ground was ready. The plants were waiting. A small number in proportion to those we grew in the other greenhouses, but still a useful one. It was, therefore, financially unfortunate that Sammy had arrived at this particular moment, for Sammy could not stay for long in the sitting room and what better place could he go than to the greenhouse?

So we surrendered the tomato plants, filled a chicken coop with hay, half covering it with a rug to give the darkness of an earth, and introduced Sammy to his new home. He was very timid, and as soon as Jeannie released him he scurried to the coop and hid himself in the hay. I do not know what else I expected him to do. He had every reason to be frightened and yet, as he hid that first time, I had a fleeting understanding of what it is that makes the unwise try to tame the wild.

I was irked by the instinct that Sammy would never be my friend. It was an affront to my goodwill. My vanity was hurt. I had a sudden anger making me wish to impel him to like me; and this, I thought, was the same unsavoury compulsion I despised in others. I should like to force Sammy to be so dependent on me that I could pretend he was fond of me. I had to surrender little. He had to surrender his life.

Jeannie patiently nursed his foot until it was well again; and when darkness fell, and there was a moon, we used to watch him running about through the panes of the greenhouse. She still fed him by hand, pushing a saucer up to him as he lay in his coop; and slowly she began to wean him from bread and milk to dog biscuits, and then to slugs. We spent a great deal of time collecting succulent slugs, but in order at first to persuade him to eat them we had to be harsh. Jeannie withheld the dog biscuits for a day so that he became so hungry that he had to taste the dish which would be one of his stand-bys when he was out on his own.

Naturally enough we had plenty of advice as to what to do with him. We should look after him for three months. We should let him go immediately. And there were the unsophisticated countrymen who, untrammelled by complications of thought, innocently proposed we should keep him for good. No subtle emotion behind the proposal. Just the plain fact that if we kept him, he would become like a dog.

What was so odd was that these blunt minds, no conscious cruelty in their stories, would proceed to tell us what had happened to other foxes which had been treated like dogs. One farmer kept a fox for three years, locking it in a pen when the Hunt was around. But one day the Hunt came on his land unexpectedly and before he had time to hide his fox, it rushed out with the other farm dogs to see what was happening; and came face to face with the hounds.

There was another fox which was happy enough with the farmer who had adopted him, which sauntered one day gaily through the front door of a neighbouring farm. He had no sense of danger. He was only doing what he had always done, being friendly. But they locked him in a room until a gun was brought.

Jeannie, who does not like to read or hear unhappy stories, would walk away and worry about what would happen to her Sammy. For he belonged to her. He would never have anything to do with me; but Jeannie could pick him up or play with him as if he were indeed a puppy. He had no fear of her, and he seemed grateful that she had nursed him back to health and strength. So it was Jeannie who was the saddest on the evening we decided to let him go.

We knew, however, that he was ready because he had been trying to dig his way under the door on the previous few nights. His foot was healed and he was big enough to look after himself, but there was the doubt as to whether he would know how to do so. Would his instinct be enough? Or would he try homing the ten miles to the earth where he came from? Or would another vixen, and there was one with cubs nearby, be ready to adopt him?

We said good-bye to Sammy, watched him slip out of the greenhouse door into the long grass, then to the side of the hedge and over the bank into the wood. And as he went Jeannie suddenly had an idea. Supposing he stayed in the wood enjoying his freedom but relying on her to feed him until he felt big and bold enough to start on his journeys? It was the kind of practical thought which softened the parting; and that night dog biscuits soaked in milk awaited Sammy's return in a saucer in the open doorway of the greenhouse.

It was gone next morning, not a crumb left; and

Jeannie was naturally elated. Sammy was being helped. Sammy had the good sense to know that he could rely on her. So dog biscuits soaked in milk were put out every night, and every morning the saucer was clean. This programme continued for ten days until one early morning, soon after dawn, Jeannie got up with the idea she might see Sammy having his meal. She didn't, of course. Sammy had never been back. He was far away by now. It was only our wishful thinking that made us believe the food had gone to him; for Jeannie that early morning saw who were enjoying their breakfast, dipping their tiny beaks into the saucer.

A family of bluetits.

It was in that early spring that Shelagh returned to Minack. She had been laid off for a few weeks by the shop in Penzance where she worked, and she came to us for a temporary job; and this time we were able to give it to her. We welcomed her with delight. For the summer-like weather had brought on the flowers in profusion, and Minack was ablaze with daffodils, wall-flowers, anemones, violets, calendulas and stocks. Here was the harvest of last year's planning and within the space of six weeks we had to win the reward.

Six weeks. There can be no neat production line on a flower farm. The results of a period of overproduction cannot be stored in a warehouse, awaiting the moment when the demand is there again. Flowers do not pause in their blooming for our convenience, nor do they hasten. Jeannie and I are at their mercy. Nor can we plan with any exactitude; for this week may be warm and the next

117

bitterly cold, holding back the flowers instead of forcing them on. Only one thing is certain, we have to clear our harvest by the end of March whatever the weather is like, for by then the great flower farms in the centre of England are storming the markets with their produce.

It was part of the charm of Shelagh that she fitted into our ways as if she had been working regularly for us as long as Jane had done. We did not have to explain to her what was at stake. She had not come to do a job of work just in order to collect a wage at the end of the week. She seemed to show that she wanted to be part of something, as if the nature of her background provided her with a vacuum which she was searching to fill.

Such a mood was understandable. She had been well brought up in a comfortable home but, however comfortable it might have been, there was no possibility of her sensing the natural love she saw others of her own age enjoying. She was illegitimate and, in a small village, there was no way of hiding the fact. Who was my father? Who was my mother? The questions must have tormented her over the years. The secret battle within her that no one could share. Perhaps the outsiders could have given her the answers. Perhaps they knew as they whispered and pitied. Shelagh on one side of the frontier, the rest on the other.

It was inevitable that Shelagh and Jane should like each other. Neither of them suffered from any pretensions and both were incapable of being jealous. Both were quiet and so neither of them would churn the friendship away by endless chatter. Indeed they were so quiet sometimes in each other's company that

Jeannie and I at first thought their silences represented disagreements. It was a foolish mistake. They were, in fact, sufficiently at ease with each other to dispense with unnecessary talk. Jane was now sixteen, Shelagh was seventeen.

But Shelagh looked younger than Jane, and Jane did not look sixteen. Shelagh was a little taller but she took away the inches of height by hunching her shoulders and walking head bent downwards. We used to tease her about it, the tease which is meant to improve a habit. 'What are you looking for, Shelagh?'

She had a little heart-shaped face with a perfect complexion, a slow smile, mischievous, a smile that she used as a manifest of her affection. Jeannie or I used to surprise her sometimes suffused by this smile as she watched a mouse sitting on her knee, sharing her lunch-time sandwiches.

She had soft light brown hair and she took much pride in it. While she worked she protected it with a grey and blue woolly skull cap with a red tassel; and on Saturday mornings before her weekly visit to Penzance she carefully set her hair and added a scarf to hide the curlers.

Her eyes were grey-blue and since her accident, when she fell off her bicycle and was on the danger list, she had to wear glasses. They were the conventional, ugly glasses and they spoilt her prettiness; and the first thing she saved up for after the flower season was over and it was decided that she should stay with us per-manently, was an elegant black pair.

She had a flair for dress and, if she had wanted to do

119

so, could have earned her living as a dressmaker. She was dainty and very appealing. When Jeannie and I saw her off-duty in Penzance, we used to say to each other that it would not be long before Shelagh was married.

She loved giving presents. She used this giving as a backbone to her life, as if here was something she could grasp firmly. It gave her a sense of security because the dates of birthdays, Christmas and Easter were on the calendar. They gave her opportunity for being appreciated and they gave her something to look forward to. All her presents were thought out well in advance.

And so were Jane's. There was one Christmas before Shelagh came when Jeremy, Jane's brother, arrived at the door on Christmas morning with a large brown-paper parcel. Jeremy, aged ten, often complained of living in a house of women, Jane and his mother; and about this time he had been helping us on Saturday mornings by washing jam jars. He had broken one or two and Jane had ticked him off when I, out of fun, said to him that I thought women were awful the way they nagged. Jeremy stopped his work, looked at me and heaved a great sigh:

'You're telling me!'

But on this Christmas morning he was at the door with a parcel. And when he brought it into the cottage, unwrapped the brown paper and then the tissue paper, we found a beautiful blue velvet cushion, piped in gold braid with a tassel in one corner; and in another, woven in red and gold, was a crown and under the crown was the letter M. As Jeremy handed it to us he bowed solemnly like a medieval pageboy.

M, of course, was the initial for Monty, and he had many a pleasant sleep on this cushion. And for Jeannie and me, the cushion remains as evidence of the happiness we shared with Jane. She had no need to spend the time, or the money, making that gift for 'His Lordship' as she always called Monty. It was a gesture of her enthusiasm and her affection.

March was a busy time for Shelagh's spirit of giving. There were two friends who had birthdays and there were Jeannie and myself; myself at the beginning and Jeannie in the middle. Even when she was in casual contact with us she used to send us birthday cards, but now she was working at Minack, and she would see us on THE day, she had to contrive to give us something that measured up to her standard of giving.

At the beginning of March, I received a box of cats' tongues chocolates. And Jane gave me something which to this day gives me pleasure. There is in the smaller of the flower packing sheds a beam which stretches across at the height of my forehead. Day after day, month after month, year after year, I used to forget that beam and walk down the packing shed, and bang my forehead against this beam. It cut me. It bruised me. It made me angry that I always forgot. And so Jane decided to do something about it for this particular birthday.

She bought a bath mat from Woolworths of a spongy plastic material, and cut it up in strips so that she was able to cover the whole beam, making it a cushion instead of an edge. On my birthday the flower shed was jammed with daffodils waiting for me to bunch, and as usual I went into it without thinking and as usual

I hit the beam. But so softly! It will always be one of my pleasantest memories of Minack when I remember the sight of Jane and Shelagh laughing at me. They had seen me through the window. They had been out picking early and in each hand they held a basket of crimson wallflowers until they were laughing so much that they dropped the baskets to the ground.

'Happy birthday!' I heard them call.

My cats' tongues chocolates were only a preliminary. Shelagh was waiting for Jeannie's birthday before she gave us our real joint present, and it must have taken her many spare evenings to complete it. I remember when I first saw it that I had a nervous reaction. It is always the same when someone gives you something which is meant to be displayed in the home, and the someone is a regular visitor. You cannot put the object away, optimistically hoping to bring it out at the right moment. Sooner or later you forget.

Shelagh had sewn and embroidered a pyjama case of black silk with pink silk lining. It was decorated with stars stitched in gold surrounding the words 'Good night' and the words 'His' and 'Hers'. And even if we had not liked it, which we did, we would still have had to keep it on our bed. For Shelagh was working in the cottage as well as outside.

In fact, I gave Shelagh to Jeannie as a birthday present. In the few weeks she had been at Minack she had proved herself invaluable. Jane hated housework. Shelagh enjoyed it; and so no wonder Jeannie wanted to keep her. And as for myself, instead of being irritated by someone dusting and sweeping in our sitting room,

I did not mind at all. I felt always at ease with Shelagh whatever I was doing. I did not notice when I was sitting at my desk that she was on her knees brushing the carpet, or at the sink doing the washing-up. Jeannie, who had done all the work herself for years, was astounded that I should be so docile. None of that: 'I've got work to do. I don't want someone in here disturbing me,' kind of attitude. I was tamed. I was the meek husband who not only was delighted that his wife was spared housework, but also made no fuss over the presence of the substitute.

One of Shelagh's tasks which gave Jeannie particular pleasure was the preparation of tea. A small task, it might seem, but in reality the drudgery of it had grown to mountain size in her mind. The custom in these parts is for the staff to bring their own tea for croust, the mid-morning break, and have a cup from the farmer's pot at lunchtime. In the afternoon they work right through to five o'clock without any break at all.

Jeannie and I, on the other hand, kind perhaps but unwise, chose to be more liberal and set a new pattern. We gave Geoffrey (Jane went back to her cottage) a jug of tea and cake for lunch, and also filled a thermos for his tea and another for Jane's with more cake for both. If we had casual labour or workmen at the cottage they received the same treatment, and cascades of tea were carried out to wherever those concerned might be.

A gesture such as this is inclined to become a habit which is taken for granted; but for Jeannie it remained a tedious chore around which the day revolved.

'Oh dear, I've run out of tea.'

'Will you fetch Geoffrey's thermos?'

'Be careful with the milk or there won't be enough.'

'I wish this kettle would boil. They're waiting.'

'I had better make a cake.'

'Will these biscuits be all right for them?'

'I must get home because I haven't done the tea.'

It was this conscientiousness of Jeannie's that Shelagh was now able to take over. She used to come into the cottage from whatever she was doing outside about an hour before lunchtime, do her cleaning, then depart with that tea. It was a merciful relief for Jeannie.

The flower season, once it starts, proceeds at such a pace that the days mingle into each other leaving one vague to the passing of time. The clock and the calendar are represented by the end of picking one variety of flower and the beginning of picking another. Thus when the meadows of Magnificence, our earliest yellow trumpet daffodil, are thinned of blooms, and then the Sulphur and then the dainty Obvallaris, I know without ticking off the days that, by being in the middle of the California and the King Alfred, we are nearing the end of our harvest, and that a month has gone by, and that in the month we have succeeded or failed in our effort to earn a living.

There are, of course, the soft flowers; and by these were meant, in the particular season that Shelagh started with us, the anemones and wallflowers, violets and calendulas, Beauty of Nice stocks, forget-me-nots, freesias and polyanthus. The sun shone down day after day, hurrying the flowers into bloom. Picking, bunching, packing, rushing the boxes to Penzance station, the volume of the work was enormous. We had no time to enjoy the loveliness of the weather. We were blind to the bursting beauty of the spring.

And these flowers also served as hour hands of passing time. First, the stained orange and yellow wallflowers disappeared into the markets leaving a miniature petrified forest where they once sweetened the air; then the Vulcan, and the dazzling crimson of Fireking.

The anemones, greedy for warmth, burst their flowers too soon, looking like pansies; and the heavy dews left moisture on the petals browning the tips, so that we would pick a basket, set them out in jars, then next morning find them unbunchable.

The stocks, sideshoots plucked day after day from the main stems, began to look like a meadow of sticks. The freesias and the polyanthus sheltered by the glass, thus cosseted in normal times from the cold, rewarded our care by resenting the blazing sun; the flowers wilted and lost their colour, the petals were soft and tired even before their journey had begun.

The violets and the calendulas gloried in the warmth; but, because they were so generous they were not wanted. There was a glut everywhere.

Then, as the flowers were consumed, as our consignments to the market became fewer, as our patience and hard work and pride were expended, we slowly began to realise our great plans of a year ago were close to failure. We had succeeded to the extent that we had a vista of flowers, no fault here in the art of growing; only the sun had defeated us. The warmest spring in many years.

Even our Cornish posies had failed us. Jeannie had started these a few years before, while I had given them their name. She had begun by using short and twisted flowers of different kinds which were unsuitable for despatch on their own; and she had gathered them into a bunch, so mingling the varieties and the colours that they became posies of delicious design. The idea was such a success, each posy was such wonderful value, that the markets began asking for more. Thus we grew flowers with the deliberate intention of including them in the posies. Wallflowers gave them body, calendulas a splash of vivid colour, anemones variety, stocks a spring-like scent, forget-me-nots a breathless blue, freesias and polyanthus another reminder to those in distant cities that spring had come to Cornwall.

The snag of these posies was the time they took to prepare. It was an art requiring patience and artistry, a careful mingling of colours and arrangement of shape. I could not do them. My efforts ended, however hard I tried, in an untidy bunch like that of a child holding a random-picked collection of wild flowers. Hence Jeannie was their creator, then under Jeannie's tuition Jane, and now Shelagh. One could go into the flower-house at the end of a day in which they had been posy-making, and the eye marvelled at the patchwork of colours that filled the jars on the shelves.

We were all in this flower-house one day, the three of them working on the posies, myself tying up the boxes prior to taking them to the station when the postman arrived at the door. As usual I quickly opened those envelopes I recognised came from our flower salesman and to my horror I saw the posies had only fetched threepence each. I was enraged, of course, because we calculated that we lost on a posy if we went below a shilling; but I was also very sad. Here around me were Jeannie and the two girls working so hard, and in my hand was the evidence that all their work was a waste of time and money. I was wondering whether to tell them when Shelagh, who had been looking out of the window, suddenly said:

'The black cat is in the stable meadow.'

At the far end, at the entrance of the gap which opens into the big field, was a spot. It was moving cautiously. It reached a patch of bare ground, hurried, then disappeared into a forest of Cromwell daffodils.

'I wonder where it comes from?' said Jane. She was clasping a half-completed posy in one hand, picking a dark-red wallflower from a jar with the other.

'Poor thing,' said Jeannie.

It had first been seen a fortnight previously by Jeannie's mother who had been staying with us. Jeannie's mother, who had given us Monty as a kitten, was out for a walk with Angus, her Scottie, when he suddenly dashed into the undergrowth barking madly. She thought he had found a rabbit. Instead, a second later, he was back on the path and ahead of him, like a streak of black lightning, was a cat. It was across a field, over a hedge and down the cliff before Angus had gone fifty yards.

The incident had no significance in my mind whatsoever. Nor, for that matter, did the occasion when I first saw the cat for myself. I had gone out early one morning, long before breakfast-time, to make an inspection of the flowers which would be ready to pick that day; and I was passing the calendula meadow when I saw right in the middle, surrounded by the blazing orange of the flowers, a tiny black head and two ears, and a pair of yellow slit eyes. The eyes watched me as I passed, the head moving imperceptibly. I was so occupied by my thoughts that I forgot to mention it to Jeannie until some time afterwards.

'By the way,' I said, 'I saw that cat this morning. It looks a bit young.'

It was perhaps natural that Jeannie should be more interested in these incidents than myself. She had always been a cat lover. Cats held a fascination for her to such an extent that any cat, however casual its acquaintance, would receive her fondling and her affection. I had had only one cat; and in any case at this particular time my mind was filled with anxiety. The flower year was ending, and the bulging enthusiasm with which I planned it was fading away into a great disappointment.

There were, however, still the Wedgewood iris in the mobile greenhouse, twenty thousand bulbs in four beds, climbing stiffly like a multitude of green spires. Here could be a lush harvest, a failure redeemed; and I remember the expert who called one day and saw them, saying to us as if he were gauging the form of a racehorse in the parade ring: 'If you can beat the Channel Islands by three days you're on a winner.'

We did not beat the Channel Islands. Indeed we did not beat anybody. The summer-like spring beat us.

For the first time in the memory of iris growers, the outside crop of iris coincided with the indoor. And we had hardly begun to pick our harvest when a telegram arrived from our Covent Garden salesman:

'Send no more. Iris up to warehouse ceiling.'

Sammy returns to the wild

8

The next time I saw the black cat it was in the chicken run. We kept half a dozen elderly hens in a clearing in the wood, protected from foxes and badgers by high wire netting, the bottom of which was buried in the ground. Nothing could jump over or dig under. But a cat could claw up a tree, leap on to the roof of the chicken house, then drop into the run below.

At one period we kept over forty hens, and the chicken house was spacious and specially designed for such a number. Jeannie had believed they would bring in some useful pin money, and they were, in fact, her responsibility. The eggs also helped, since we lived so far from a shop, to make the daily catering easier for her.

We found, however, as others before us, that the pin money was an illusion and that so much was paid out every week on expensive laying pellets that it was cheaper to buy the eggs. Thus gradually the flock was thinned out until these six old pensioners were left. Very occasionally one of them would lay an egg; but the real justification of their existence was based on sentiment.

They each had an identity of their own. The prospect of killing them was out of the question.

I had gone along one morning to open them up when I saw the little black cat inside the run by the chicken-house door. For a second it stared at me, motionless, then it ran, racing across the run in panic, until it hit the wire netting at the far side. Foolishly I went after it. I do not know what my intentions might have been but my approach increased the cat's terror and it began clawing at the wire and attempting to thrust its head through the mesh. I suddenly realised it might strangle itself. The head might just possibly get through a hole, but its body, thin though it was, never. For an instant I put out my hands as if to pick it up. The threat of such help from me made it instinctively recoil from the netting; and the next moment I saw it take a flying leap on to the chicken-house roof, up the tree, and down again on to the ground outside the run. It disappeared into the wood behind.

From now on one of us saw the cat almost every day. Sometimes one of the girls saw it when they were picking wallflowers in the sol meadow at the top of the cliff. Another day Shelagh found it in the lane as she was bicycling to work. Jane once frightened it on the path leading to her cottage. And there were numerous times when Jeannie or I spotted it in one of our fields or in our wood. Indeed one of the strange things about its activities was that it was always on *our* land; and yet our land dovetailed into that of my neighbours in most complicated patterns. It kept within Minack boundaries and spurned the others.

But none of us could get anywhere near it. It ran away at the sight of us, although on occasions it sat on a hedge on the far side of a field, watching; a little black spot in the distance. And there were other occasions when it chose to sit in the lane about a hundred yards from the flower-packing shed, the other side of Monty's Leap, as if it were trying to make up its mind to come nearer.

I was still too busy to take much notice of it. I was worried. The income from the flowers was far below expectations. The reserve I hoped for did not exist; the work had been done, the wages paid out, the bills incurred, and here Jeannie and I were at the flower year's end without a penny available for our own endeavours. We had both worked for nothing.

Defeat, or danger, is easy to face when it is met suddenly for the first time. One feels elated that the secret self is being challenged. Here is the chance to bring out the hero, the somnolent section of one's being that longs to justify itself in the dramatic. But I always feel that the very nature of the courage that is required on such occasions is deceptive. It looks like courage while in fact it is an emotional outburst. It can be, indeed, a form of showmanship. In times of sudden danger or defeat one can be so intoxicated by excitement that one is scarcely aware of one's actions.

The aftermath of such courage is when real courage is needed. The gesture has been made but the danger has remained, and a hangover has taken the place of exultation. One now slips into a remorseless delaying action, a tedious clinging to hope; and one is forced to realise that factors have to be faced which provide no stimulus. They are the factors of repetition, the further defeats, the further dangers, leading one on and on until suddenly comes the day one discovers that despair has replaced the struggle for victory as the enemy.

In the kind of life we had chosen it was Jeannie who was tested when promise was unfulfilled. She had left behind in London so much that earned the envy of others. As the Public Relations Officer of the Savoy Hotel Group she was at the top of her profession. She had a large salary and expense account. She was able to mingle with the famous and live a life that had the trappings of a film star. Her office, as she described in her book *Meet me at the Savoy,* was the meeting place of household names. It was used as a club. At any time you might find there Danny Kaye or James Mason or A. P. Herbert or any of the top newspaper correspondents; and she was described by an American magazine as 'the prettiest public relations officer in the world.'

She thus had standards by which to judge the value of her present life that were not ordinary. Moreover she knew that if she so wished she could return to London and live again the sophistication she had surrendered. At any moment of doubt the glamour was beckoning. The gaiety was waiting. She could forget the water which had to be pumped from the well, the paraffin lamps, the endless cooking, the long hours of bunching, the cold wet days picking the flowers, the naked simplicity of her existence. She could leave all this behind. She could look back and call it a time of folly. She would not be the only one who wanted to escape, then found escapism too tough, and returned.

Yet she never did consider such an alternative. I never had to listen to her telling me how wonderful things once had been, or could be again. Nor did she put doubt into my mind that I might be demanding too much of her. Instead it was she who gave me the courage. I count myself tenacious but I do not enjoy taking risks. I foresee trouble before it arises and so I can argue myself out of taking bold action. Jeannie on the other hand, acting by instinct, will stride into a situation undeterred by reason; and once embroiled she does not retreat.

Here we were then at the end of March and our only aid was tenacity. It was, as I have said, something I understood; but both of us were weary. Every problem, however simple, was therefore huge. And any solution required the melancholy prospect of starting again the same pattern of growing as the previous year when our hopes had been high. We had, in fact, gambled and lost. We had also, as the result of our gambling, become more involved in the mechanics of living from which we had set out to free ourselves. We could consider ourselves no longer as escapists. We now had responsibilities of a parallel nature to those we had left. We had created dependants. The lives of Jane, Shelagh and Geoffrey were bound up with ours.

It was now that the little black cat became a pleasant diversion. It haunted Minack to such an extent that Jeannie and the girls began to taunt me for taking so little notice of it. I was accused by them of all the anti-cat inclinations I possessed before Monty came into my life. I was being obstinate and cruel. Here was a little black cat that was so obviously seeking affection, but I was not even offering to help it overcome its terror of human beings. Here was an example, they said mockingly, of anti-cat brutality.

'He's heartless, isn't he, Mrs Tangye?'

'The poor little thing is starving.'

'Let's wait until he's gone to town and then we'll feed it.'

It was pleasant to be laughed at in this way. It relieved the tension. It helped me to see my problems in perspective. It was foolish to let myself indulge in depression just because I had been disappointed, and was tired, and because I suffered from the sickness of wanting success quickly. I was meeting again my old failing, the belief that endeavour on its own is sufficient to gain material triumph. I was ignoring, as I had done before, the rewards I had won. My eyes were staring at a pedestal so far in the distance that I was blind to what was close to me, the small pleasures which sparkled at me, the glory of awakening every day to an environment I loved. I had no right to demand more than this. The beat of my life was within the truth that men can look for all their lives; and fail to have the luck to find.

Easter was early that year. At the beginning of the week I saw my friend Walter Grose walking through Minack on his way to hoe potatoes in his part of the cliff. Walter for many years had worked one of the three farms whose buildings straddled the top of the hill and through which we passed on the way to the main road. He had now amalgamated his farm with that of Jack Cockram, the young man I had been able to introduce to my landlord. Walter and Jack made a good combination.

'How are you today, Walter?' I asked. And he replied in his usual way with his warm smile;

'Poor but happy.'

But I had a reason other than pleasantries in talking to him that day. Walter had a large assortment of farmhouse cats which roamed his outbuildings and it occurred to me that the little black cat might be one of them. It wasn't. He had seen it himself down at Minack, but he had no idea whence it came. Why didn't I ask the travelling fish salesman?

I had the luck to see this gentleman in his van later on in the day when I was going into Penzance. Once a week he visited every farm in the district and the cats always hastened from their hideouts whenever he appeared. At each farm they grouped themselves round the open van doors as he displayed his wares to the farmer's wife; handsome toms, battle-scarred ladies, cats of every colour and description. He was the most popular visitor of the week. He was the cats' friend. He knew them all. No one was better placed than he to tell me whether anyone had lost a little black cat. But he could not help. I saw him a week later and he still could not help; and by then he had made special enquiries at every house on his round.

Meanwhile Jeannie, Jane and Shelagh had been active. They waited until I was out of the way, then put down a saucer of milk a hundred yards up the lane; it was just at the spot where the little black cat was in the habit of watching us. An hour or so later the saucer was empty.

The next time they did this I caught them red-handed. They believed I had gone down the cliff to look at the potatoes, and so I had, but I returned quicker than they expected; and I found Shelagh, followed by Jeannie and Jane carrying a saucer of bread and milk into the old barn where Monty used to hide when he first came to Minack. It was the Saturday morning of the Easter weekend.

'I know very well what you're up to,' I said, and I felt angry, 'you're trying to make that cat stay here. I won't have it!'

I was repeating myself. I had said the same thing about Monty. Here was the simmering again of my pro-dog and anti-cat childhood. True, I had loved Monty, but there were exceptional reasons why I should have done so. He had been with us in a turbulent period of our lives and he had reflected to me the comfort of security. I had never become a slave to his species as Jeannie had done. I remained suspicious of cats in the mass and I was not going to have another one just because a stray seemed to be in need of some milk. Yet, and this was lurking at the back of my mind, what were my last words to Monty? Did I not talk about a black cat?

The little black cat lapped up the bread and milk though it waited until there was no one about. Jeannie looked in the barn during the afternoon, found the saucer empty and promptly refilled it.

'Look Jeannie,' I said after she had done so, 'I appreciate your feelings but you must try and appreciate mine. I don't want another cat. For one thing we can never expect to have a cat again which doesn't catch birds, and for another I want to keep my independence. After all even with Monty we were pretty tied down looking after him.'

I was aware that my words sounded hollow to her. Indeed I don't think she even listened. She had ideas of her own so she thought it more convenient to let me ramble on.

'I'm thinking of Charlie and Tim,' I said, 'and all the other birds which now trust us. Are you really prepared to risk their lives by pandering to this stray cat? I can't understand it. And you know perfectly well that if you go on feeding it, it will want to stay.'

I was particularly concerned about Tim. He spent so many hours of every day on my desk or on the back of a chair or perched high on the top half of the stable-shaped front door. He would warble a song, or go to sleep on one leg, or just observe. And when we went outside and we wanted to show him off to a visitor we would shout for him at the top of our voices; and within a few minutes he would wing his way to us, and I would hold out my hand for him to perch on. He was unperturbed by strangers. He was so trustful that it was dangerous; and, having trusted Monty, would he not trust any cat?

Charlie, I felt, could probably look after himself. He was a forceful character, always on the move and, in the spring and summer, a very noisy one. He would end-lessly cheep at us and sometimes he got on my nerves and I would yell to him to shut up. Indeed this noisiness was to prove his undoing. He never had the good sense to know when to stop; and there was to be one day when he went on too long. But I did not foresee this on that day when I was telling Jeannie I wanted nothing to do with the little black cat. Nothing at all.

I do not know how long I would have maintained this tough attitude; but the following day, Easter Sunday, something happened which bewildered me. The condition which I fancifully made when Monty was dying was fulfilled. It happened in this way.

About eleven o'clock in the morning Jeannie was sitting in the chair opposite the fire, reading to me her diary of the year before in which she described her earnest efforts to help Monty in his illness. It was a wild day, and perhaps this influenced her to become somewhat upset. I felt distressed for her because she had always secretly believed that she might have been able to have done more than she actually did. This was untrue, of course. Nothing could have saved him.

A tremendous storm was blowing and as I often do when this happens, I switched on the trawler waveband to hear what the ships thought of the weather. The unknown voices came over the air from ships I would never know, and yet so frank, so intimate were these voices that I felt I could have taken part in their conversations. Suddenly I heard a cry at the door.

'Did you hear that, Jeannie?'

One can imagine cries in a storm, or cars arriving, or planes overhead. When the gales blow I am always saying that I hear someone shouting, or Jeannie believes someone has roared down the lane in his car, or I am imagining an airliner in trouble. This is what happens when you live in isolation and there are no standardised sounds of civilisation to measure against unreality.

'I thought it was a miaow,' said Jeannie.

And it was.

I opened the door and there was the little black cat huddled outside in the rain. It did not wait for me to invite it in. It rushed past my feet into the room, and sat itself down at the foot of the bookshelf which hides the sink; and waited there, as Monty had always done, yellow eyes looking up at Jeannie for the saucer she was only too ready to give it.

What was I to do? It had acted according to plan. It had fulfilled the conditions. I had put up a resistance, as indeed I had done when Monty was produced to me at the Savoy as a kitten, but the situation was beyond my control. How could I deny a home to a cat that had come to Minack in such a remarkable way?

It was a female. The vet who dealt with her said she was about three months old. He took her away, performed the necessary operation, and when we collected her she purred all the way home. A dainty little cat, totally black except for a wisp of heart-shaped white on her chest, and with a pretty little head fit for a chocolate box. We never knew where she came from. We made exhaustive enquiries within a radius of ten miles in case she had indeed been loved by someone, and then lost; but not a soul knew anything about her.

We were warned that she would not stay with us. A cat born out in the wild, and this must have been the explanation, always returns to the wild. A wild cat, in fact, is always a wild cat. That is what we were told.

But she is still with us today, three years later, and she is over there now curled in the corner of the sofa, plump and as glossy as a ripe blackberry. I cannot believe she is the same little black cat which hurled itself against the wire netting of the chicken run.

And her name? She is called Lama, after the Dalai Lama who was at the time escaping from Tibet.

Geoffrey, meanwhile, had accepted the sparring which preceded her arrival with solid calm. He had tolerated the interest shown in the cat, but his mind was on his work. He lived in his own world. And I do not think he really approved that girls were working along-side him. He had spent his life making use of his brawn; always on the cliffs, always turning ground, or shovelling potatoes in or shovelling them out, or digging up bulbs or planting them again. His was a world of muscle and long-established traditions. It was a fading world and he had, as it happens, the intelligence to know it. The shovel was a dying instrument and the shovel man was going the way of the horse. The reign of the cliffs was over. Science was replacing brawn. All of us who depended on the little meadows that stared out at the sun and the sea, that for generations had rewarded those who toiled in them, were trying to adjust themselves. Jeannie and I were intellectually aware of this. Geoffrey sensed it. That was the only difference between us.

He was away for seven weeks that spring, first in hospital and then convalescence; and I was on my own again as far as the heavy work was concerned. It was the time of tomato planting, of soil preparation and seeding, and then of potato lifting. Most of my waking hours were spent driving the big tractor, ploughing and cultivating the ground, or using the lurching rotovator or, when May came, stabbing my shovel under the potato plants with the girls and Jeannie picking up behind me.

We only had a half-ton of seed that year; and it was the last year we ever grew potatoes. We had planted them in the meadows of Minack cliff which we had cut ourselves when we first came, a patchwork of meadows of deep soil and high hedges, secret meadows that a stranger would not find unless he was led, meadows so small that you might wonder why they were there. Each one tilting towards the sea, each one so designed to receive the greatest possible protection from the anger of the wind, from the clammy poison of the spray. That was the idea and the hope.

I remember the first of those meadows. We still lived in London but Minack had become tentatively ours in the sense that our friend Harry Laity allowed us to be his tenants. We travelled down whenever we could for a few days; and on one of the earliest visits Jeannie and I became childishly excited because we found a pocket of ground which obviously, long ago, had been a cultivated meadow.

It was right at the bottom of the cliff, edging the last drop to the sea; so when we stood in the shadow of its once-cared-for cultivation, we could look down on the waves when the tide was high, or on rocks and shallow pools when it was low. On one side there was an ancient stone wall, on another a high elderberry hedge; and in the centre was the meadow itself, chest high in undergrowth yet seemingly shouting at us to recognise it. Ghosts were there. Old men with sickles, blazing sunshine, parched soil, gulls' cries, tempests raging, forgotten harvests, a wren's song, badgers playing, the scent of primroses on soft spring mornings. We saw this hint of a meadow, and for a glorious two days Jeannie and I with the insane urge of enthusiasm ripped the undergrowth away, broke up the roots, and before we hurried back to civilisation, stared at the sweet earth, thankful for its reality.

Jane loved the potato season, though heaven knows why. Doubtless it was because she was unencumbered by the financial considerations by which Jeannie and I were always judging its progress. We were always worrying whether this meadow or that had had a good yield; or raging because the morning's post had brought news of a bad drop in prices. My aches brought on by the digging became worse on such occasions, and the half-hundredweight bags when I carried them up to the top of the cliff felt as if they weighed half a ton.

Jane said she liked the sensation of the soil running through her fingers as she searched for the potatoes. She would be on her knees, barefooted as usual, scratching away at the ground like a badger, then call out that she didn't think much of my digging. It was an old joke of the potato season.

'You'd better catch some fish, Mr Tangye. We've got plenty of chips!'

And by this she meant I had been careless, that I hadn't dug deep enough under the plant, and the shovel had cut the potatoes in half. Then, a few minutes later, I would get my own back. I would thrust my shovel into the soil a few yards behind her, and find a potato or two which she had failed to find and pick up.

'Has the picker-up gone home?' I would ask.

An endearing feature of both Jane and Shelagh was the loyalty they had for the crop. Thus, even when we had a poor day's digging, they would report in the evening that we had had an exceptionally good one. There was, of course, fun in doing this. At potato time the parish used to seethe with rumours about the quantities, quality and price of the crop on the various stretches of the cliff. Jane and Shelagh liked to stimulate the belief that Minack cliff was doing particularly well. Jane, for instance, had a malicious pleasure in teasing her mother's boss.

This farmer had grown early potatoes for years on the cliff not far away, and he prided himself on always being the first to send them to market. He was a taciturn chap who took life very seriously; and it was easy for Jane to spread in his mind alarm and despondency. Thus she would naughtily tell him at a stage when he had not sent away anything, that I had sent away a twelve-pound chip basket; when, in fact, Jeannie and I had only eaten our first plateful of new potatoes. And then, as soon as the season got under way and he regularly asked her how we were doing, she used to double, even treble, the amount of the day's digging. She would also add salt to the wound by exaggerating the price.

'We dug twenty-two bags yesterday,' she would tell him cheerfully.

'You did?'

'Yes, and we're getting a shilling a pound.'

'You are?'

The farmer would lugubriously look at her, fumbling

in his pocket for a packet of cigarettes. Then he would turn away, ruefully wondering whether she was speaking the truth; and next morning she would tell me gleefully what had happened.

Shelagh was too shy ever to be so bold; and in any case, as she was a new hand at picking up potatoes on the cliff she was not conversant with our brand of potato wit. She would hurry on with her work, never pausing, and if she talked it would be about her previous evening's bicycle ride, or Russ Conway; she was mad about Russ Conway.

Her bicycle rides were phenomenal journeys in view of the fact she had already done a day's work; and at weekends she would go on marathon trips with her girlfriend Pat, who worked in Penzance. Twenty miles in an evening, forty miles on a Sunday. And on Saturday afternoons she always had a long session at the cinema, two complete shows for the price of one ticket was her aim, and it did not matter how fine was the weather. This, in fact, became a joke.

'Well, Shelagh,' one of us would say on a Saturday morning when the sun was burning us all, 'a really wonderful day for the pictures!'

'Yes,' she would reply, grinning, and delighted we had made a joke of it, 'a really hot day to spend in the dark.'

All through the time we were digging the potatoes it was blazing hot. Jane's hair got fairer and fairer and her skin browner and browner. When a meadow was too small for the three of them to be behind me picking up, Shelagh and Jeannie would stay with me while Jane went off on her own to another meadow. She took the spare shovel which was as tall as herself, and then would vigorously plunge it under the plants. She would get very hot and dirty, smudges of soil all over her face, and then at lunchtime she would suggest to Shelagh that they go down to the rocks to bathe. But Shelagh, who incidentally was always as spruce at the end of the day as she was at the beginning, would be shy at the prospect.

'Isn't it funny,' said Jane to Jeannie the first time, 'Shelagh was quite shocked when I took off my clothes to bathe.' Jane, I do not suppose, had ever owned a bathing suit in her life.

The wonder of these two, each in a different way, was that they were untamed; and they belonged to the cliffs as the badgers and foxes and the birds belonged. They had no edges carved by sophistication, they had no brittle rainbow ideas to lead them away from their happiness. Their eyes and minds were alert for pleasures which, one might say, did not belong to their time.

I remember the delight with which they heard my story, during that May, of how I saw a fox running along the rocks within a few feet of a lazy, lapping sea. I had gone down the cliff to bring up a few potato bags which we had left there the evening before, when I saw a fox stalking a gull at a spot a hundred yards away where the grey rocks met the green landscape. I had shouted soon enough to warn the gull, and it flew off, but the fox without hesitation dashed towards the sea and then, as I watched from above, skipped like a ballet dancer from rock to rock until it disappeared from my view behind a turn of the cliff.

There were also that May two litters of fox cubs all of us were able to watch grow up. One litter had an earth at the top of the cliff in a bank that sloped from the big field to the meadow where our Soleil d'Or bloomed in the early spring. There were three cubs and they used the sol meadow as their playground, flattening the dying leaves in their gambols. They were not easy to watch. A hedge hid them from the field side, and a stone wall from another. The only convenient point was to peer through the elderberry trees that divided the sol meadow from the one in which we grew Rembrandt daffodils. From here we used to watch their antics; and it was here that Shelagh used to come in her lunch hour, then tell us of the laughter they had given her.

The other litter salted our pleasure with constant concern. They were not on our land and so they were not safe from a gun like the others down the cliff. The earth was in the corner of a field across the shallow valley from the cottage, so placed that we could lie in bed and see it through the open window. There were five cubs and their parents had been obstinately foolish to dig the earth where they did. For they had been warned in previous years that their presence was not required. They would open up the earth and then, a few weeks later, the farmer would stop it. He quite rightly could not allow a valuable field to be used as a playground.

But this year the farmer had done nothing; and there were the cubs every day chasing each other all over the field while the proud parents sat side by side and watched. They could, of course, see us plainly and hear our voices, but they seemed to think there was some kind of magic to protect them from danger. I could shout at them and all they would do was prick their ears and stare in my direction. Fear did not exist; and the parents, who in normal times lived with fear daily, were so dazed by the happiness of possessing such cubs that they forgot to teach them the wisdom of fear. We had it instead, on their behalf.

The farmer kept a large number of chickens and he naturally had to keep guard over them. He had already taken steps to control the badgers, and one of our worries was that he might take the same kind of steps with our foxes. He had engaged the pest control officer to block up the holes of a large badger sett, and the badgers had thereupon been gassed. Such a method is perhaps merciful, though most countrymen will tell you that only rogue badgers kill chickens.

We now were concerned that the reason why this year the farmer had failed to stop up the earth was because he had decided to wipe out the litter. If he stopped the earth he knew about, they would only go to another he might not know about. So perhaps his idea was to let them be for a while, and then either gas them or shoot them one by one.

Thus every day we expected the wondrous sight of the cubs at play to end; and I was scared what Jeannie might do if she saw the slaughter taking place. She was certain to see it if it did. The cubs, as we watched them from the cottage, had become like pets. We had names for each, and each so clearly had a character of its own; as happens whenever you watch animals for long.

We began to fear every early morning and every

early evening, for then it was that the shots would most likely ring out. And so we found ourselves looking at the gambolling cubs, while watching the undergrowth cover which surrounded the field . . . in case we saw a man with a gun.

Our anxiety became absurdly out of hand. We began to worry so much for the cubs that we forgot to enjoy the pleasure of watching them. And yet was our anxiety so absurd? Farmers are unpredictable because they act for the most part according to mood; and adjoining moods can be gentleness and violence. Farmers, in distant parts, can possess the sly instincts of a cornered animal; and thus their actions cannot be trusted. One moment they murmur good wishes, the next howl in distress, or perhaps what is more unsettling, they will nurse a grievance without giving you a clue what the grievance is about.

It was Jane who decided what we ought to do. It was unwise, we all agreed, to ask the farmer what his intentions might possibly be; for it would draw attention to what was happening, and there was still a chance, since the field was distant from his farm, that he did not know. So Jane decreed that we should subject the cubs, and their parents for that matter, to our particular brand of danger. If we took the right measures they would all shake off their halcyon confidence, and yet be saved.

And that is what happened. We imposed fear on them.

When they came out of the earth to play we banged dustbin lids together; and when they got used to this noise one of us used to run up to the gate of the field and clap our hands together. Slowly, by these methods, the cubs became aware of fear; and their parents remembered it.

It was during this period that I realised that Hubert, the gull on the roof, was ending his reign as king of the roof. He could no longer squawk for all other gulls to fly away. He, instead, would fly away himself at the screaming demand of an insolent stranger. I was perturbed.

And then one afternoon, an afternoon when we had a particularly good crop of potatoes, Jeannie came calling for me in anguish.

'Hubert's been shot . . . been shot.'

Derek holds Lama

9

I found Hubert on the cedarwood top of the coal shed where Jeannie always fed him. He was standing on one leg. The other was hanging limply, and blood covered the webbing of the foot. Every few seconds he staggered, hopping an inch or two, his wings unfurling and flapping, trying to keep his balance. He still looked as regal as ever and he was glaring at us; as if he were in the mood of one who was cursing himself for the mess he was in, like an old man who had at last lost his independence.

'What have you done, old chap?' I asked, 'what's happened?'

'He's been shot, I tell you,' Jeannie answered for him angrily. 'I was standing here when he came down and I saw quite clearly a bullet hole through the webbing of his foot.'

He had always been more Jeannie's bird than mine. He tolerated me, he squawked at me when he saw me and when he was hungry, he had even come for walks with me, gliding up and down above and around me with the grace of a swallow, but he never awarded me the honour of feeding him by hand. He shied away when I proffered him a morsel. He was nervous of me.

But he was at ease with Jeannie. She used at first to feed him on the roof of the cottage and she soon learned that he required bacon rinds or her own home-made bread. So she would throw whatever it was up on the roof and if it fell short of him, he would slide down to it, using his feathered posterior as a toboggan. This was a comical sight.

Then, as his confidence grew, he decided that the coal shed with a top like a table and situated a few feet from the door, would be more convenient. It was here that Jeannie fed him by hand. She would come out of the cottage calling him, and he would swoop from the roof or the top of the great stone chimney where he had been ruminating, and seize what she was offering him. And when he had gobbled it, he would strut the small space, imperious, impelling his personality upon her so that she weakened, saying: 'Hubert, you've had enough . . . but here's one more small piece.'

Sometimes he was in such a hurry to come to her that, if the wind was blowing, he made an error of judge-ment in his landing. He hated it when he made such a fool of himself and, after recovering, he would sail into the sky like a flying god, majestic wings outstretched, with a symmetry of body that made our hearts beat in excitement. Here was the wild that linked the centur-ies, noble, remote, free and yet gloriously tempting us to believe we shared something with him. Here was a thing wiser than man, luckier perhaps because it was not fooled by greed. It was content with the splendour of living. It embraced the sky and the sea and the rocks, struggled with the storms and gloried in hot summer days; it was a speck against blue and a crying, swerving, rebellious being that pointed black clouds, shining them by its white, uttering far distant calls, telling us who were ready to listen that the gale was coming again; the same gale, the same gull, the same human beings since the beginning of time.

Yet Hubert also provided the moments of absurdity. There was one occasion when Jane was with us and Hubert got blown by a gust of wind so that he was poised for a second just above Jeannie's head. It was a ludicrous sight. I was beside Jane and I knew why she burst into laughter. Jeannie, for that second, looked like a lady who had searched hard for an original hat; Jeannie who never wore hats.

'You must go to a fête with Hubert as your hat, Mrs Tangye,' laughed Jane, 'you would be a sensation!'

There may have been another reason why he chose the coal shed as his dining-room table, beside his growing confidence; and that reason was Gregory, the one-legged gull. I always presumed that Gregory had lost his leg in a trap. In the terrible days of the gins, gulls – when storms blew and they settled for the night inland instead of on the rocks – would guilelessly choose a field which was ringed with traps; and the inevitable would happen. I do not see how else he could have lost his leg.

We called him Gregory after Gregory Peck, who at

the time was making the film of *Moby Dick* and playing the one-legged captain. We had no particular reason to do so, it was just that the name seemed to fit. And so whenever one of us saw him sail down on to the apex of the roof we would call out that Gregory was here; and quickly tend to his wants.

We had to be quick because Hubert did not like him, nor did our other occasional gull visitors. The hate was so strong and Gregory's fear so great, that we used to see him in the field across the valley, a speck against the green, watching, waiting until the roof was clear and he could safely visit us.

He would arrive usually at twilight, and when we had appeared and seen him, he would flutter down to the coal shed and hop about like a man with one leg but no crutches. But only for a minute. Then, having gained his sense of balance, he would wait there motionless except for his head which would follow us as we came out of the door with the delicacy we had chosen for him.

'Here you are, Gregory,' and we would toss him a piece of meat.

Then, having got it in front of him, he would look up into the sky. He was always on guard. He was always expecting attack. He was always frightened that the hindrance of one leg, which made it so slow for him to take off, would result one day in his being caught unawares.

And it did. I do not know when or where it happened but there came a day when he did not appear, then another; then a week, then a month. We never saw Gregory again.

There had been occasions, however, when Hubert had caught him on the roof or on the top of the coal shed having a meal. Hubert was enraged. He had no doubt been somnolently basking on a rock when the idea occurred to him that a snack at Minack would be pleasant; and he would sweep in from the sea and find Gregory already enjoying one.

Hubert would scream his fury, diving at Gregory, who would desperately try to escape; and always did. But Hubert on these occasions behaved like a bully and we obviously gave him no sympathy. He was jealous. Minack was his kingdom. And we had the effrontery to feed someone else. And in a different place. It was from the moment when he first caught us in the act of feeding Gregory on top of the coal shed that he decided to use it himself.

Poor Hubert. For months we had observed how he had been ageing, how he himself was often attacked and then chased over moorland towards the sea by one of the brash young gulls who wanted to usurp his place on the roof. The old tale of the wild destroying the old. The inevitable conquest of youth. And there was nothing we could do except watch and be sad. Hubert was receiving the treatment he used to give to others. And now, like his old enemy Gregory, he was standing on one leg on top of the coal shed. Who had shot him?

I could see the hole quite clearly, an airgun pellet, I guessed. It was a neat opening and it appeared that the pellet had gone right through the foot. There was blood, but no swelling as far as I could see; and Jeannie pointed out hopefully that when she first saw him he had, in the effort to keep his balance, momentarily put the foot down. The bones of his leg, therefore, were certainly not damaged. We were staring at him anxiously when he suddenly decided that he had had enough of our attention. He gave us one more glare, then heaved himself into the air and flew off, seemingly as independent as ever. We watched his flight, and it was so powerful that we found ourselves thinking we might be worrying unnecessarily. We ought to be thankful that he had escaped with his life. A miracle, in fact, that he had done so; but we felt enraged at the thought of the person who had aimed his rifle at him as he peacefully stood on a rock by the sea.

The next morning Jeannie and I were up early waiting to tell Shelagh and Jane. Something so pleasant about these two was the prospect of seeing them every day. They were usually sleepy for the first hour or so, silently pursuing their duties in a daze, but by ten o'clock they woke up. They began to talk. And if there were subjects of mutual interest to discuss, I used to wait until that hour to discuss them.

On this particular morning, however, our news shocked them into immediate wakefulness. They loved old Hubert, and they would always be telling me something they had seen him do; chasing another gull or himself being chased, or telling me as if I hadn't known it already that Hubert was squawking his head off, and asking if one of them should go and feed him. Hubert was as much part of their lives as he was of ours.

They too were, of course, enraged; but Jane had

also some important information to impart. Jeremy, her young brother, apparently had an indignant row with some boys who had been walking along the cliffs the previous day. And the reason for the row was because they carried air guns and were taking pot shots at any gull they could see on the cliffs. It seemed to be plain that Hubert had been one of their victims.

Why is it that airguns and .22 rifles can be used without licences by anyone of any age? Why are parents so callous as to allow their children to have them? It is a streak of stupidity and brutality that I will never understand. No doubt it is due to lack of imagination; and as a result birds and animals are killed in the name of pleasure, a pleasure which masquerades as sport.

We next saw Hubert at lunchtime. He flew around above the cottage for a few minutes as if he were wondering how best to make his landing; and as he did so I called the girls so that they too could see his wound and make their comments. He hovered for a moment or so above the roof, then came down gently, and made a perfect landing on the coal shed. As he did so he put out his foot as if he had forgotten it was hurt, then immediately retracted it; so there he was glaring at us on one leg.

He was otherwise unperturbed that the four of us were close to him; and in any case he was far more interested in the juicy pieces of chopped roast beef that Jeannie had kept for him. He began to gobble so quickly that he had to pause and stick up his head, so that we watched the meat bulging down his neck and throat. He certainly had not lost his appetite.

157

'What do you think?' I said, 'What shall we do?'

I was appealing to their instinct which I felt would be surer than mine. My intellect, in times of distress, becomes mixed up with my emotions, creating a confusion in my mind that flusters my ability to make decisions. Jeannie knew this, and the girls guessed it, so my request for their opinions was not really necessary. They had already, without intent to offend me, decided to ignore my views; not, as it happened, that I had any to offer.

The questions to answer were these: how serious was Hubert's injury? Should we try to catch him and keep him somewhere until he was fully recovered? Should we catch him and take him to the Mousehole Bird Hospital? Should we take the chance of letting him live on among the rocks and seas he knew so well, feeding him with special delicacies in the meantime, trusting that he would best stage a recovery in these natural surroundings?

The speed with which Hubert had devoured his meat influenced the girls and Jeannie into believing the injury might not be so bad. There had been time for the reaction of shock. He could have been listless. If it had been really serious, he would not have wished for any food at all. Hence they decided to let him be for the while; and, needless to say, to keep a special watch out for him.

He came regularly for the next four days, and he seemed neither better nor worse. Jeannie had made a special visit both to the butchers and the fishmonger, and had also doubled our weekly order for bacon from the St Buryan grocer. Hubert, even if he lacked an appetite, was to be tempted to have one.

It was on the fifth day that he made a foolish mistake. In a moment of overconfidence, or perhaps it was touching evidence of the trust he had in us, he settled on the apex of the roof as if he were roosting. He was up there like a pigeon having a sleep on a branch. I had never seen him do it before, his habit had been to strut on the roof, up and down, up and down, like a sentry. But there he was, white chest puffed out, enjoying a rest in the sun; and I felt afraid that it would only be a matter of a few minutes before one of his rivals would see him.

Sure enough from the direction of the Carn which stands upright like a monolith above Mount's Bay, a half-mile away, I saw a speck speeding towards us in the sky. Nearer and nearer it came across the moorland with the inevitability of an express train. I guessed it was Knocker, Hubert's particular enemy; and so named by us because whenever it wanted attention it would bang its beak on the roof with the rat-tat-tat of a woodpecker. A few seconds and it was over the stables and poised for its dive of attack.

'Hubert!' I shouted, clapping my hands, 'Look out!'

The old bird looked round just at the instant that Knocker, screaming his war cry, swept past him within a few inches of his head. I picked up a stone and threw it at Knocker who was now high in the sky again, wheeling, a beautiful murderous savage, ready, ready to dive again.

I saw Hubert gathering himself together, like an old

man trying to rise from his chair; but instead of standing he slipped, then slid down the roof to the gutter which halted him for a second before he overbalanced, and fell like a half-opened parachute into the garden. Up above Knocker cried out his triumph.

Jeannie arrived at this moment. She had been somewhere in the wood and heard the noise, and guessed what was happening; and as she rushed past me Hubert staggered a few feet down the path, then managed to collect himself, heaving himself into the air, so that we were able to watch him together struggling to keep airborne, skimming the stable roof by a few feet, then over the may tree that borders Monty's Leap, towards the moorland and the sea. And all the while Knocker was sweeping round him, twisting and turning above and beneath him, escorting him like a triumphant fighter pilot beside a crippled bomber, taking him further and further from the safety we could have given him.

'I should have caught him when he fell,' I said angrily. I was cursing myself for failing to react instantly. I had gaped like an onlooker at an accident. Had my mind not been so ponderously dull, I could have held him in my arms within a few seconds of his falling; and we could have looked at his wound, and nursed him, or taken him to the Bird Hospital. It was a failure I would always remember.

'Next time he comes,' I said determinedly, as if words would compensate me for my feelings, 'we will catch him and . . .' I added, doubts about my ability to do so brimming again, 'you, Jeannie or one of the girls had better try and do the catching.'

But Hubert never did come again. A gale blew up that night and raged across the sea from the south, surging the waves on the rocks where Hubert used to shelter, tearing with the sound of tube trains round the cottage, doom in the noise, so that Jeannie and I lay awake talking and wondering and afraid; and in the morning the gale still blew, and it was so fierce that even if Hubert had been well he would have stayed away from the cottage. He always used to stay away in a storm; and then, when we saw him again, swooping down from the sky to perch on the roof, we used to say a prayer of thanks. Rage had been expended, peace had returned. Normality had replaced cruelty.

Jane said it was lucky I had not caught him. She believed that as he had lived along this stretch of the cliffs all his life, it was better that he should die at some point along them. He would have died in any case cooped up in a cage.

'He died free,' she said. And there was wisdom as well as comfort in her words.

It was the middle of May and a sizzling summer lay ahead; and as the sun beat down parching the soil, denying germination of seeds, drying up the wells, killing transplanted plants, burning us all as brown as South Sea natives, I found no peace in what the holidaymakers called a wonderful summer. Once again we were laying the foundations of another flower season, yet we were being hindered from the beginning. There was threat in the sun and the blue skies. We could not have another year of failure and still hope to keep

161

Geoffrey and the girls. We wanted rain as those in the desert want rain; and it never came.

The anemone corms, which in normal times would peep green shoots within ten days, were as hard and dry as nuts six weeks after sowing; fifty thousand corms lying dormant which had to puff out sturdy plants by late September if they were to stand a chance of blooming through the winter. And ten thousand corms which I had failed to lure into growing by soaking them first in water, were dead. The root tendrils, deceived by my cleverness, had pushed out into the dusty soil and, finding no moisture to sustain them, had withered away into nothingness.

But it was the wallflowers which tested our patience the most. We succeeded in germinating them, in nursing them through the stage when weevils and flea beetles attack them in dry weather, in growing them to hand-high plants ready to bed out in their winter quarters; and then the trouble began. Poor Jane and Shelagh. I admired and pitied and was grateful for their endeavours, but I rebelled against helping them. I preferred more congenial tasks. I spent endless hours watering the freesias, for instance, dangling a hose from my hands vacuously watching the spout of water darkening one section of soil, then another. But I refused to help Jane and Shelagh, although Jeannie did occasionally when she could spare time from the tomatoes. The desperate slowness of their task, the vast number of inevitable casualties, the apparent threat that the wallflower crop had already failed before even it had begun to flower, depressed me into inaction. I did not want to see what was happening. I preferred to believe the problem did not exist. Let Jane and Shelagh get on with it. I could trust them to do their best.

And perhaps the wonder of their loyalty and their enthusiasm was the way they struggled on day after day with this transplanting of twenty thousand seedlings. So many have a task and give up when the task challenges their tenacity. It is easy to be excited about a job which is new, or when the end gives quick reward. Here they were faced by a huge field of hot dry soil, so hot that even Jane complained on some days that her bare feet were walking on hot cinders; and into this hot field they had to bring alive again, after digging them from the seed beds, the early-flowering wallflower upon the success of which so much of the flower season depended.

Each had a pail in which they mixed soil and water until it was a muddy mess, and each seedling was dipped into it. They wrapped the mud around the roots so that there was a cocoon of moist mud. A monotonous job. Hour after hour, day after day; and in the evening Jane would report to me the number that had been planted.

'A record, Mr Tangye,' she would say, proud that they had indeed planted more than ever before, 'we've done twelve hundred today!'

Twelve hundred, it wasn't much. But they had first to dig up the seedlings from the seed bed and this, using a trowel, was a tedious business. The ground was hard like cement, and their hands blistered, and their wrists ached from the jab of the trowel as it scooped out the long tap roots. They were always so meticulous. They never made a show of doing a job. Slipshod did not belong to their vocabulary, and so if progress was slow it was never time wasted. They both aimed for success in everything they were ever asked to do, not for some flamboyant gain; just for the sheer personal pleasure they gained from doing their best.

They were lucky, I suppose, in that they both had a feel for flowers, and a love of the earth, and a communion with blazing suns and roaring winds; and they had minds which found excitement in small things, the sight of a bird they could not identify, or an insect, or a wild plant they had found in the wood. They were always on the edge of laughter, of pagan intuition, of generosity of spirit. They were not cursed by the sense of meanness, of jealousy of others, of defiance.

They wanted to love. There was so much in life to be exultant about and I never knew either of them, even in fun, say a harsh thing about anyone.

And yet Shelagh, I feel, suspected the identity of her mother. Indeed she may have met her once, although as a stranger, when she delivered a note to a house in the village where visitors were staying. And there was another time when Shelagh, looking for somewhere to live, was inadvertently given the address of her mother by someone; and Shelagh wrote innocently asking if there was a room to spare. There was not.

These incidents, for all I know, may have happened while she was at Minack, and others as painful as well; and this would explain why there were days in which she appeared silently to sulk and be moody, days on which Jane, Jeannie and I would work hard to win from her that delicious grin.

'What's wrong, Shelagh? Cheer up!'

'I'm all right.'

Jeannie and I were not so foolish as to pry into these moods ourselves. We left it to Jane. And Jane was too subtle ever to bring the mood to bursting point by asking too many questions or by appearing self-consciously aware that something was wrong. If the first approach was turned down by Shelagh, she did not persist. They would work alongside each other in long silences, comfortable silences, and then I would look again and see them chatting to each other, and I would know that Shelagh's mood had passed.

'What was wrong?' I would ask Jane later.

'She didn't say.'

Both of them were secretive and why not? It is impertinence, I think, for those with experience to question the young. The young are a race apart with magical values and standards, with mysterious frustrations and victories, free from repeated defeats, fresh, maturing, bouncing into danger, propelled by opposites, frightened, confused by what is told them. And their lecturers, I believe, are those who, having failed in the conduct of their own lives, recoil to the hopes of their youth, reliving ambitions by pontificating, hurting the sensitive young and being laughed at by the others. Experience should be listened to by the young. It should never be inflicted on them.

Even in high summer Shelagh would be thinking

of Christmas, and if one of us wanted to enliven a moment of the day, Shelagh would be asked:

'How many days to Christmas?'

'One hundred and twenty-seven.'

'Did you hear that, Jane?'

'Yes, and I bet she knows what presents she'll give already!'

Shelagh spent the year planning these presents but this coming Christmas was a special one for her. It was the first year that she had earned a wage above subsistence level, and she confided to Jeannie one August morning when she was busy dusting the house: 'I've always promised myself that I would give the most wonderful presents possible to all those I love at the first Christmas I had the money to do so.'

One of our presents from her that coming Christmas was a picture of Lama sitting on the white seat by the verbena tree. Lama, because she is all black, is a most difficult subject to photograph; she dissolves into all normal backgrounds. But Shelagh, noting this, waited one day until Jeannie and I had gone out and lured Lama to sit on this particular white seat and took the photograph with her box camera. The photograph was taken in August and she did not tell even Jane; and the secret was hers until we undid the coloured wrapping and found Lama, eyeing us, in a neat frame.

Lama loved her. Lama, because she had been born wild, did not know how to play and Shelagh set out to teach her. It was extraordinary how, in those first months, we could dangle anything in front of Lama, or tease her with a twig, or play the games associated with cats, and receive no response whatsoever. She just didn't understand what we were trying to do.

But every lunch hour, if Shelagh's pet mouse had not arrived before her, Lama would sit on her lap as Shelagh munched her sandwiches, taking any portion which was offered her and then, as if paying her bill, would tolerate the efforts of Shelagh to make her play; a piece of raffia tickling her nose or a pencil pushed between her paws. In time, with our help as well, Lama woke up to the pleasure that cats are able to give human beings.

Shelagh was phlegmatic towards animals and birds, and yet touchingly loving. If, for instance, I expressed concern at the prospect of Lama coming face to face with her pet mouse, Shelagh would appear quite unperturbed.

'My mouse would hide in my shirt.' And she said it as if it were the most ordinary thing in the world that a mouse should hide in a girl's shirt.

And yet I sometimes saw a ghoulish side to her, a macabre sense of humour which relished an unsavoury situation. I remember once coming into the flower-house and finding the mouse on her shoulder while Lama had entered the door ahead of me.

'Look out, Shelagh,' I said.

She gave me a wide grin, showing no anxiety whatsoever.

'Just think,' she said lasciviously, 'if Lama *did* catch Patsy how wonderful her crunches would sound!'

She delighted in murder stories and the more gruesome the better. And so sometimes, when work progressed and we felt in the doldrums, one of us would sparkle a minute by telling Shelagh that we had read about a particularly brutal death in the papers; and her eyes would light up in mock excitement.

'Tell me more!'

And then, if the facts themselves were not horrific enough for her, we would invent some that were; and we would all end up sharing the same ghoulish laughter.

This apparent callousness was, of course, superficial, though I suspect it was also a form of armament. She was afraid of her own gentleness, and she needed to bolster herself sometimes by pretending she was tough. She had to prove to herself that she was independent. She was not a rebel in the sense that she had a chip on her shoulder; she was just tired of always being under an obligation to others, and she wanted to have her own personality and be free.

She had a wonderful way with sick birds, a fearless, uncomplicated tenderness towards them. There was one morning when she arrived half an hour late and instead of bicycling she had walked.

'Had a puncture, Shelagh?' I called, as I saw her coming up the lane. Then I noticed she was holding something under her coat, and when she came up to me she showed me a wood pigeon. She had found it lying on the side of the road a few minutes after she had started out for work; and so she had gathered it up and, because it would be difficult to carry if she bicycled, she had left the bicycle behind.

We took the pigeon straight away to the Bird Hospital at Mousehole. Its wing was broken after being shot, and a pellet had to be extracted. In due course, however, the wing began to heal and the pigeon regained its strength; and there came a day when Shelagh received a note from the hospital that the pigeon had been set free. She was brimming over with happiness, and from then on whenever a pigeon passed overhead she used jokingly to call out:

'There's my pigeon!'

She once had the extraordinary experience of working in one of the greenhouses when a merlin hawk dived through a half-opened ventilator, landed at her feet, and knocked himself out. Heaven knows how he managed to do it or what he was after, but there was Shelagh peacefully weeding the tomatoes when she suddenly felt a rush of air, heard a plomp, and saw on the ground beside her an inert bundle of feathers.

It so happens that birds seldom fly straight into the panes of a greenhouse from the outside. They swerve away in time. Indeed I have only known the gloriously coloured bullfinches appear blind to glass; but they, thank heavens, are migrants in this part of the world. I do not often have to pick up their beautiful bodies.

The trouble starts when a bird goes into a greenhouse and does not know how to get out and in its panic hurtles itself against the glass until it is senseless. Oddly enough it is usually the yellowhammers which are the victims. Time and again I have found a dead or dazed yellowhammer. A wren is far too nimble-minded ever to hurt itself and although wrens seem permanently to haunt the greenhouses both in winter and summer, I have never seen an injured one. Robins usually ignore our greenhouses and I never saw our Tim in one, although he was happy in the cottage. Thrushes, too, do not venture inside. But the blackbirds have a glorious time when the tomatoes are red and ripe. They gorge on the fruit, earning our curses, but we are ready to give them a tomato in return for a song.

Shelagh treated the merlin in the same way she and Jane always treated the dazed yellowhammers. She filled the cup of her hand with water, and in it she dipped the merlin's beak, opening the beak with her fingers so that the water trickled down its throat.

It is an astonishingly quick way to stage a bird's recovery. There it is resting in your hand seemingly helpless . . . and you have the sweet pleasure of watching it slowly come to life. You are alone with it. It is quiet. You feel the tiny claws tickling, then touching, then clutching your hand. And then suddenly when all kindness has matured, it is away . . . towards the wood, up into the blue sky, or down along the moorland valley. Here is triumph. Here is truth.

And because the merlin fell by Shelagh he did not have to wait to be helped. Had he chosen a moment to perform his miracle of escape when the greenhouse had been empty, hot, dry, unfriendly to anyone or anything which was injured, he would have died. But Shelagh was there to save him. And she could not keep the victory to herself. So when the merlin began to show life again, and Shelagh knew the danger of moving him was over, she brought him to us in the cottage.

'Look at this,' she said with her delicious grin, and the merlin clasping her hand with his claws. He was awake now. He knew he was alive. He would go soon.

But he stayed long enough for me to get one of the bird books so that I could read out its identification: 'Upper parts are slate-blue, the nape and under parts warm, often rufous, buff, the latter with dark streaks.'

It is such a moment which quells worry, and in a wondrous flash transforms depression into exultation. There I saw before me not only the majesty of a bird returning to the wild but the stream, the clear, sparkling stream, the dawning stream of a girl's happiness. If only it could have remained for ever.

Both of them had the same stature. Jane, like Shelagh, had the mind which instinctively helped the helpless. Here were these two at Minack, sustaining Jeannie and me with the glory of enthusiasm. In this place we loved so much were these two who shared the pleasures we, so much older, felt ourselves. The young voices calling for their hopes amongst the gales and the rain and the heat. So far to go. So passionately willing to give to the present.

Jane was always more sure of herself than Shelagh because she had been loved for herself, since she could remember. And yet, in her way, Jane was as vulnerable. She loved the weak; but when she demonstrated this love she liked to dispense an atmosphere of drama. It was fun to do so. And so it was in this mood she arrived at her work one summer's morning and disclosed an exciting piece of news.

'Mr Tangye,' she said breathlessly, 'a Muscovy drake spent the night in my bedroom. We want to find a home for him. Can he come to you?'

*The photograph of Lama which
Shelagh secretly took*

10

The Muscovy drake had arrived in a sack brought in the back of a car by a young farmer who aimed to make himself popular with the Wyllie family. He could not have created a worse impression. Jane, Jeremy and their mother would have starved rather than eat it.

It was magnificent. It was a large white bird, the size of a goose, with dark green feathers on its back, a powerful pink beak with a red bobble on it bridged by two holes like nostrils, huge yellow webbed feet, an angry red skin beneath the white feathers of its neck and head, piercing, intelligent eyes, and the ability to raise the crest of feathers on its head when annoyed, like the fur of a furious cat. It could also hiss like a steam engine.

Jane brought it across the fields from her cottage in her arms, unperturbed by its apparent ferocity, and she arrived at our door as if she were holding a Ming vase. I looked at it apprehensively.

'And what, Jane,' I asked, 'is the procedure for looking after a Muscovy drake?'

She was grinning at me. She knew I had felt a little

irked by being forced to agree to accept it. I had not been in the mood to collect any further responsibilities. I had dallied when she offered it to us. I foresaw difficulties. What about foxes? What about it flying away and all the hours we would have to spend searching for it? I saw it becoming a tedious tie, not because I would dislike the bird; on the contrary, I knew I would grow too fond of it. And I felt at the time that I did not relish such a worry.

'Oh, it's quite simple,' said Jane, talking to me as if I were a backward small boy, 'it'll be quite all right in the chicken run with Hetty.' Hetty was our one remaining chicken. She lived in a large chicken house by herself, and occupied the day pecking in the extensive wired-in run in the wood.

'Surely Hetty won't like being chased by a drake?'

'You're quite wrong,' said Jane with a sweet smile, 'the drake won't show any interest in Hetty at all.'

Here Jane, in due course, was herself proved to be wrong. The drake and Hetty developed a strong platonic attachment and when Hetty, due to old age, began to fade away, the attention of the drake was touching to watch. For the last two days of her life he never left her side. They remained together in the chicken house refusing to come out. Nor could he be tempted to eat anything.

Jeannie, naturally enough, did not share my hesitant views. The prospect of helping another creature delighted her. She is one of those people who would fill the fields with old horses, the house with stray cats, and leave a legacy to provide grain for the birds on the bird table.

'We must have a pond for him,' she said within twenty-four hours of his arrival at Minack, and I observed that 'it' had already become 'him'. 'The postman,' she added, 'told me this morning he was certain to fly away to look for a pond unless we do something about it.'

There happened to be a drought. Springs were so low that we had scarcely enough water for domestic use from one well, nor enough for our tomato or freesia seedlings from the other well. The idea of making a pond was an impossible one.

'It's up to you,' said Jeannie in that tone of voice which I knew would mean she would get her way in the end, 'if you want him to fly away . . .'

The idea of his flying away was a threat that hung over us for a long time. People seemed to have a malicious pleasure in telling us this would happen. Cut his wings, they said, or you'll lose him for certain. But we did not want to cut his wings for fear of frightening him. We did not want to upset him. We wanted him to feel at home and to trust us. In the end he never did fly away, that is for any distance. He flew, a magnificent beating of his wings, but only round and about the cottage. The prospect of touring the district in search of him never materialised.

I suppose it was the pond which restrained him, although the pond in the end was only an old tin bath just large enough for him to splash in. And he owed it not to Jeannie or me or the girls, but to Julius. We were at our wits' end how to make his pond when Julius found the tin bath thrown away in the undergrowth near the cottage.

***

Julius was one of those sixteen-year-olds who seem to mature before their time. He was on holiday from his school in Switzerland and staying not far away. We had known him off and on since he was a child, and one day this particular summer he had suddenly appeared at the cottage. He was good-looking, erudite even for an adult, and effortless as far as Jeannie and I were concerned. He had a restless wish to be alone on the cliff, and he would come to us, have a meal and then go off down to the rocks by himself; and later I would find him there staring out to sea.

'What are you thinking about, Julius?'

And in reply I would have a penetrating commentary on world affairs, or a more personal outlook on life. One did not think of him as younger than oneself. One had with him a standard of conversation like playing tennis on the centre court at Wimbledon. The ideas bounced back at one another with speed.

As soon as he found the tin bath he dug a hole in the chicken run, the exact size, so the rim of the bath was on a level with the surrounding soil; and then he carried water to it until it was filled. We waited expectantly for the drake's reaction and in due course he waddled towards it, dipped his beak into the water, and a minute later was sitting in it looking like a battleship in a small lagoon.

'Well done, Boris,' said Julius.

'Why Boris?' asked Jeannie.

'Well he must have a name and as he is a Muscovy he ought to have a name which sounds like a Russian.'

The Muscovy breed does in fact come from America but Boris sounded good. We all agreed upon that. It had a solid quality about it, tinged by the mysterious, which suited his personality. We had already seen enough of him to realise he was a determined bird who would develop set ways with strong likes and dislikes. He also obviously had intelligence. He would stare at us, not with the vacant expression of a chicken, but as if he were summing us up. It amused us.

'What are you wanting, Boris?'

'He likes being talked to,' Jane would answer for him.

After Hetty died we thought he might be lonely. We considered finding him a mate and some people said he would go off and find one himself unless we did something about it. But a mate would mean eggs and eggs would mean baby Muscovy ducklings and as there would never be any question of killing them we decided to risk him going on an amorous quest. He has never done so. He has remained a bachelor and never given a hint he would like it otherwise.

He lives alone in the big chicken house, a house that was built for fifty hens. Every evening as dusk falls he waddles off to bed, a flat-footed walk with his whole feathered body wagging from side to side, a measured walk of habit, the same route every day, the soil packed hard by his webbed feet; we have given up trying to grow anything on his route to the chicken house. And when he arrives he roosts on the perch like a chicken, and waits for one of us to lock the door.

'Have you put Boris to bed?'

'Not yet.'

'Well I'll do it.'

Most evenings there is this scrap of conversation at Minack; for we are on guard about Boris. He is a tempting target for a fox or a badger. We hurry home to put him to bed, plans revolve around him. We do not feel at peace wherever we are if we know the chicken-house door is still open.

And in the morning we act in reverse.

'Get up. It's time Boris was let out.'

I envy those who are able to treat pets casually as if they exist only to titillate man's boredom. I envy them their harshness. They can pursue their relationship with birds and animals on a metallic basis, a scientist's standard. Emotion in their eyes is a vulgar thing. The heart of a bird or an animal does not exist and so they can treat them like a new toy, gloriously loved on its arrival then simmering into being a nuisance, then back again at intervals to being loved again.

Love for an animal is no less than love for a human being. It is indeed more vulnerable. One can compose oneself by the assurance that a human being can evict disillusion by contact with his friends. But an animal yields trust with the abandon of a child and if it is betrayed, shoved here and there, treated as baggage or merchandise, bargained over like a slave of olden days, everyone except the cynic can understand the hurt in its eyes. But the cynic grouses that we who see this hurt are suffering from a surfeit of sentiment, the word which the cynic parades so often as if it were his fortress.

I prefer, therefore, to behave indulgently to those who depend on me and who, for that matter, respond to my attentions without deceit. Hence Boris seemed to us from the beginning worthy of our minor sacrifices. He gave us pleasure and so we were glad to repay him.

He was puzzled by Lama; she had shed her wild disposition with remarkable speed, and she was now a homely cat, a cat who liked to sit on my knee wasting my time as Monty had done. She showed no wish to go out at night and instead chose to lie curled at the bottom of our bed, not taking up much space for she was a little cat. She had become very trusting, perhaps foolishly so. She appeared to be bewildered by the love that had suddenly come her way. She worried us, for instance, by her careless attitude towards the danger of cars. She always hurried to hide under any which were parked outside, and when we returned home in the Land Rover she would plant herself in the middle of the lane and refuse to budge. She was also insensitive to the threat of Boris's fierce beak.

I think it understandable that Boris should have been jealous. We may have fussed over Boris but Lama, in comparison, was pampered. Boris used to eye us picking her up and hugging her, and although Boris would come for walks with us he did not like to travel far from the cottage; then he would stop and crossly watch Lama continue at our heels, a cat which had more enterprise than a drake.

Thus, whenever the opportunity arose, he liked to show his displeasure. He used to make feint attacks on her if she came near him, outstretching his neck, waving his head like an angry snake, hissing, waddling menacingly towards her. And because Lama in her wonderment believed no one could dislike her she would remain still, watching him come nearer and nearer, and only sidle away at the moment when I was about to shout her a warning.

Boris was always particularly vexed when he was having a meal outside the door of the cottage and Lama was wanting to come in or go out. We fed him on scraps and more especially Jeannie's home-made bread, though his favourite was the leftover dough with which she had made the bread; like the gulls he would have nothing to do with shop bread. He had, of course, the grass and undergrowth to sift for insects, the freedom, in fact, to go where he wanted, but anything he found on these searches was considered by him to be either an hors d'oeuvre or a savoury. He insisted on the square meal that we were able to provide for him and every so often during the day he would pad up the steep path to the cottage.

As we threw him the scraps he would wag his tail feathers in pleasure, and gasp a strange noise like an out-of-breath man. This display of contentment would continue unless he caught sight of Lama poking her black head round the door or coming up the path from behind him; and then he became alert and angry and instead of soft gasps there were hisses.

Lama, on these occasions, responded with caution; a sensible cat who appreciated the rage she had engendered. She was sorry about it and she looked at Boris as if she were telling him so. There was certainly never any sign that she wanted to meet anger with anger. She was meek and mild. She just stared at him, waiting for the moment to slip by when there was the minimum chance of a peck from his beak. Perhaps she considered herself a superior being, a being that could sleep on a bed, not perch in a henhouse. A different social level. A snob. Perhaps she thought it beneath her dignity to take any notice of such raw ill-manners. And yet I doubt that this was so. I am sure she was fond of Boris and enjoyed his companionship. Why otherwise, as I often saw, should she turn on her back, paws softly curled, inviting him to come to her in the way she invited us to play with her?

Jeannie and I felt towards Lama the same kind of affection we felt towards Shelagh. Both were waifs. Lama came into our lives from the unknown, a lost wild kitten of the Cornish cliffs, while Shelagh, yearning for love, came from the barren land of no true parents. They had this forgotten quality in common and it helped no doubt to create the affection they showed each other. And I was glad, therefore, that Shelagh was there on the one occasion when Lama was in trouble.

Charlie the chaffinch had been with us so long that we knew his appearance with the same detail as one knows the Union Jack. And we had observed during the previous few months that he had developed a bump on his head just above his eye; and then after a little while we noticed the eye begin to close until in due course Charlie was making his monotonous call as a one-eyed chaffinch. We were of course very upset but there was nothing we could do. He was impossible to catch. He also continued to be as gay and thrusting as usual. He was the dominant figure of the bird table. He was the echo which followed us around. And yet we realised he was nearing his time. A healthy chaffinch, a young one, would not have a blind eye. And after all, had not Charlie been with us for eight years?

He used to annoy Monty as the wrens used to annoy him, chirping around his head from a bush as he lay somnolent underneath. He did the same with Lama. I can understand this annoyance, because if you are suddenly awakened from a deep sleep by a noise that flushes you into momentary bewilderment, you are usually for an instant bad-tempered. You say something which you afterwards regret. I have never hit anyone, though I have cursed them.

Lama was sleeping under the stunted apple tree just opposite the cottage when Charlie chose to perch on a tiny branch just above her, and began yelling his monotonous call. I was fifty yards away at the time but Jeannie was lying on the grass nearby, reading a magazine when, for an instant, she put it down, and saw to her horror that Lama had leapt at the branch and swiped Charlie into the grass.

She cried out: 'Derek! Derek!'

I had a sick feeling of disaster, and I rushed to her, murmuring those phrases which are aimed to quell distress; 'All right, all right, I'm coming!'

Charlie had recovered from the blow of Lama's paw sufficiently to fly to a branch of a nearby elderberry.

It was soothing to see he could fly.

'Now don't worry,' I said to Jeannie, trying to give myself confidence, 'Lama could not have hurt him. He flew perfectly well to that branch.'

I could see him half hidden by the green leaves, chest

182

puffed out, absolutely still, facing towards us and I could sense his astonishment that after all these years of haunting us, of bellowing his harsh tuneless cry into our ears, that we should have turned on him. I suddenly felt angry.

'What did I say?' I said, taking it out on Jeannie, 'what did I say would happen if we let Lama stay?'

Mine was an outburst which was foolish and unfair. It was nobody's fault, and yet I was ludicrously, self-ishly lashing about for a scapegoat. How could I dare blame Jeannie? Or Lama for that matter? It had been one of the miracles of Lama's time at Minack that she, like Monty, showed not the slightest interest in birds. The initial suspense as to how she would behave had disappeared from our minds. I had seen her many times sitting in the garden, dozing or washing herself, while Charlie or Tim or the others bobbed around the flowers looking for grubs. She was a gentle little cat. Only mice stirred her hunting desires.

I was ashamed, a moment later, of my outburst but this was no time for apologies. We had to find out how badly Charlie was hurt. He was sitting there on the branch as if he were frightened to subject his wings to the test of flying away. I had never seen him remain still for so long.

'We'd better try to catch him,' I said.

I believe, in retrospect, that my real intention was to assure myself that he was all right. I was wanting to catch him not so much as to help him as to prove to myself that help was not needed. I wanted to see him move. I wanted to create the belief that our fears were false. I wanted to advance on him and relish in the glory of his escape from me, seeing him beat his little wings as he always had done.

Yet I knew he would be frightened of me. He was not like Tim. He had never become domesticated. He had never dared come indoors or stand on my hand as Tim did. And yet, remote as he might have been in comparison, he belonged to Jeannie and me. We could call for him, and he would come. We could go a mile away from the cottage and suddenly find him beside us. He had attached himself to us as a mascot, always friendly, but always elusive.

One autumn he disappeared and after a month or two we gave up hope of ever seeing him again. It was natural to think he was dead and as the winter passed and there was still no sign of him we forgot about him. And then one morning in early spring Jeannie went into the wood to feed the chickens when suddenly she was startled by a familiar monotonous cheep just above her head. There was Charlie on a branch. Charlie in magnificent spring plumage. As boisterous as ever. And Jeannie was so excited that she rushed to tell me, forgetting to feed the chickens. He never went away again.

'You stay this side of the elderberry,' I said to Jeannie, 'and I'll go the other. Then we can converge on him together.'

My intention, if he stayed still, was to let Jeannie catch him. When she was a child she wanted to be a vet, and she had the compassion and gentle touch of those whose ambition is to relieve suffering. She had the courage too, to grasp firmly and not to dither at the instant when calm is the key to success. We advanced.

As soon as we moved I knew we had made a mistake. For he took fright, and tried to fly, but instead of flying this time he fluttered like a falling leaf in a breeze, over a stone wall and down on to the lane which lead to Monty's Leap and the stream. It was a mistake in that we now knew he was badly hurt; we could no longer watch him and hope.

'I'll try again,' said Jeannie. And she went carefully forward calling him.

We now knew that it was vital to catch him if he were to be saved; and yet each time Jeannie came near to him he fluttered away from her again. He would rise a couple of feet from the ground, then struggle a flight of a few yards and down again, spreadeagling his tiny body in a tussock of grass. He was treating us as his enemies. He had no trust in us. We who had received such joy from him over the years were being refused the chance to repay him. The long familiarity of his perky presence, the countless times we had, in mock anger told him to shut up, the delight of his sudden appearance on a walk, all these memories were dissolving into the climax of his life, a climax in which he was doing all he could to evade our help.

He was now three-quarters of the way down the lane; and the stream, and Monty's Leap, were only a few yards from him. We suddenly thought there might be method in his fear of us, and that he was seeking water for the same reason we gave water to dazed and injured birds of the greenhouses. We stood still. Three minutes went by. Five. Then Charlie fluttered again, and with an immense effort, half flying, half running, he dumped himself at the stream's edge on the side of the lane where it dashed on through undergrowth and moor to the waterfall which splashed to the sea.

'Look,' said Jeannie, 'he's drinking.'

He was dipping his little beak into the water, so alertly, with such an air of brisk sense that both of us had a wave of thankfulness. Impossible, it seemed to us at that moment, that a bird which was really ill would behave in such a manner.

'Somehow,' Jeannie said, 'we *must* pick him up. As he is he won't last the night – an owl will get him or a rat.'

It was afternoon. Indeed a Sunday afternoon. And we both found ourselves wishing it was an ordinary day. Then the girls would have been with us and we could have discussed the next moves, and we could all have shared the understanding; the understanding that is so absurd to some, the understanding that gives reason to the determination to save a bird's life.

'There are two people coming down the lane.'

I said this as I have often done, with a note of apprehension. There is no right of way through Minack but we seldom mind people passing by. In an age when transistors and cars anchor the holidaymakers in car parks and packed beaches, it is refreshing to see those who have the initiative to walk. Nine times out of ten the walkers are delightful, and how strange it is that they are so often foreign students and teachers. It puzzles me how it is that, looking at the brochures and preparing their holiday plans, they come to the decision of walking this lonely coast. It pleases me. It is only the map-makers who distress me; only the neat-minded folk who look for trouble, badgering farmers who in the process of earning a living block up a gap to stop the cattle escaping; and then are ordered to open it again to allow rare crocodiles of organised walkers to scurry on their way. Even in this untamed land there are those who wish to spoil it. The busybodies. Those who will never be able to understand solitude. For it is the solitude, I have found, the total freedom from signposts and selfconscious man-made paths which attracts the visitors who pass Minack. In this crowded, over-organised world they have found peace in this stretch of Cornwall which has been spared the planners.

'Who are they?'

It was essential that we should not be interrupted in our vigil. If two brash walkers came by, ignorant and insensitive to our task, Charlie would become more frightened than even we had made him.

And then suddenly we saw it was Shelagh. Shelagh and Pat, her girlfriend who lived in Newlyn. No purpose in their visit. Just the inclination for a Sunday afternoon walk along Minack cliffs. A lucky coincidence that led them to us at the exact moment we needed Shelagh most. Jeannie and I were so pleased to see her that she was startled by the reception we gave her.

'Why do you think I can help?'

Yet she knew. We did not have to answer her. This was one of the occasions which she would look back upon, revelling in it, rejoicing in the proof that she was needed. She knew she could catch Charlie. There was this primitive, uncomplicated kindliness about her which would permit her to go straight to him. There would be no doubts in her mind to make her hesitate. She would go forward, bend down, and pick him up. As easy as that. And that is what happened.

We put him in a small box of dried grass in a warm corner of the greenhouse. He was very weak and both his eyes were now closed. There was nothing we could do to help him and in a few hours he was dead. A little silent bundle of feathers.

The next day Jeannie wrote a rhyme:

Dear Charlie, we teased you much about your voice
That sharp, shrill cry.
But how today we would rejoice
To hear you call against the sky.

And having buried him at the foot of the same tree on which he had greeted Jeannie that spring after he had been away, we went down to the cliff meadows. We wanted to be on our own for a little while. We went into a meadow which lies directly above the sea guarded by a low old stone wall. We sat on the grass, the sea before us blue as the Mediterranean and behind, hedging the opposite side, the blazing yellow of the gorse bushes. We had been there for a few minutes when suddenly we were startled by a familiar cry. A monotonous cry. And there, just above us, was a chaffinch perched on a gorse bush.

'This is unreal,' I said to Jeannie.

But it wasn't. It never left us for the half-hour we sat in the meadow, and when we returned to the cottage it came with us, chirping all the way like the yap of a small dog. From then on it took Charlie's place and although it did not possess his boisterous nature and was more timid and not nearly so thrusting on the bird table, we felt that the uncanny way it had replied to Jeannie's rhyme had earned it a worthy name. He became known to us therefore as Charlie-son.

Jane, at this time, was enjoying a passion for music and one day she proudly announced that she had become the owner of a house-sized Wurlitzer organ.

'Now, Jane,' I asked, 'what does that mean?'

One of her charms was that she skated between the serious and the comic; and so when she made this announcement I was a little on guard whether or not she was strictly speaking the truth. She was such a glorious enthusiast that she deserved to be given a lee-way in her remarks; for I know myself if I am exulting over some idea I may have had, flushing its prospects with exaggeration, that I resent a listener quelling the sense of it by logic. It is wise to be foolish some-times, to experiment, to court mistakes; for one cannot embroider personal achievement in any other way. One remains sterile if one always plays safe. It is essential to be mad on occasions.

'I ought to call it a harmonium,' she said, looking at me and smiling, 'but a Wurlitzer organ sounds better.'

Heaven knows what prompted her to buy it. She couldn't even play the piano, or any other musical instru-ment for that matter. I think perhaps the idea began with a romantic picture of her sitting in the cottage, the win-dow open, answering the roar of the sea and the cries of the gulls with the volume of her music; and mingling all the sounds together in a hymn to her happiness. Whatever the reason it was not a practical one.

The harmonium had spent many years in a Wesleyan Chapel near Camborne until, worn out, it was bought by a dealer who repaired it, then sold it to Jane for nine pounds. It was a bargain price, and he topped it by offering to deliver it free. Poor chap, he did not know the problems ahead because after travelling the long lane to the cottage he found the door too small for the harmonium; and he had to take it to pieces, carry them into the cottage and put them together again.

'And now,' said the man, his task completed, wanting a musical reward for his pains, 'let me hear you play.'

Jane sat down, pounded the pedals with her feet, and crashed out some most unharmonious chords. She did this, apparently, with élan; indeed she behaved according to character. She could not play a note but she wasn't going to admit it. She possessed, in fact, courage.

We were given the account of this incident early the following morning when we were cutting lettuces. It was a solemn period of the day. The lettuces had to be delivered at Jacksons, our wholesalers in Penzance, by half-past eight in the morning; and as Jane lived nearest she used to come in early to help us cut and pack them. She was usually three-quarters asleep.

'Jane, you dormouse, wake up!'

There was a routine in which Jane could play her part automatically, in a daze. I used to go up and down the rows pinching the hearts of the lettuces and cutting those which were full. Jane would follow along after me picking up those I had cut and carrying them back on a tray to Jeannie who was on her knees, surrounded by lettuce crates, cleaning each lettuce of its dirty leaves, then packing them twenty-four to a crate.

The sight, in a small way, was impressive when ten crates were full and Geoffrey, who had arrived by this time, was loading them in the Land Rover. But were they worth the trouble? In an age when time-and-motion experts reduce the prospects of reward for most endeavours to decimal points of profit, I hesitate to believe that our lettuces rewarded us.

Look what had to happen before the housewife bought one. The ground had to be prepared, the fertilisers scattered, the seeds sown, the seedlings thinned out, watering going on all the time, hoeing, probably a battle against greenfly, and then the climax when they were ready for harvesting.

'I've a fine crop of lettuces,' I would say to Jacksons', 'how many would you like?'

Having pursued the struggle of growing them and having poured out the cost, a grower when asking this question is in the same mood as a prima donna before an opera performance. He is tensed.

'How many?'

'Oh well,' comes the answer, 'the public are not buying lettuce. Say ten dozen.'

Jeannie and I have spent many hours of our lives standing in the forecourt of Jacksons' store on the front at Penzance discussing lettuces with Fred the foreman or one of the Jackson brothers.

'Surely you can take more than ten dozen?'

'We can't sell what we've got, old man. Honest we can't.'

'I've run out of crates, Fred.'

'Hang on a moment, I'll get you some.'

'When shall I come in again?'

'Make it Friday, early as possible, old man.'

This is the tedious part of growing. The part I do not envisage when the seeds are sown; then all my hopes and concern and endeavour dwell on the struggle to produce the crop. I am blind to the time when I have to sell, when the results of all the hard work depend on the unpredictable whim of the public. My cocoon of pleasure that is wrapped around the achievement of growing a fine crop is now torn to shreds. I am back again in the metallic world from which I sought to escape. I must be a businessman, and bargain and argue and flatter; and I must be prepared to face the fact that what has been produced is not wanted.

And then, perhaps the day after I have returned to Jeannie in gloom, I get a message from Jacksons': 'Bring in as many lettuces as you can.' The public, overnight, have acquired a taste for lettuce. A miraculous force has gathered them together and marched them to the greengrocers. Nothing rational about it. Nothing that even the most experienced could foresee. Just a whim.

Sometimes on these summer mornings when the Jackson order was a big one, Shelagh would come in early too. And there were occasions when Julius would also proudly arrive.

'A record walk this morning. Clipped a minute off my time.'

His was a wonderful walk. He was sleeping in a caravan in the woods of an estate a couple of miles away; and the route to Minack was across green fields that were raised like a plateau above the sea, then down into a valley where a stream rushed in haste, leaping the boulders, sheltered by a wood where foxes hid, bordered by lush vegetation in summer, and in winter welcoming snipe and woodcock giving them a home safe from the guns. Julius loved this walk. He crossed the valley, then up past Jane's cottage and over the stone hedges to Minack.

'Heavens, Julius, I didn't expect to see you today.'

'I thought I might be able to help.'

He would always quickly go and have a look at Boris because, I believe, he was proud that he had named him. There was, for always, a link between the two. It may not have been very important, but then I sometimes wonder how to gauge the degrees of importance. I have remembered many things, which at the time outsiders would have considered insignificant.

Julius was one of those people who, youthful though they may be, instinctively wish to help others. It is not just the question of practical help. It is the art of conversation, or of silence; the intuition when to continue a line of thought, or when to stop. There are no lessons to be given about these things; the sense of embarrassment which for a second may be hinted, or the flicker in eyes which give a clue to secret hurt, or the flavour of a moment which insists on a change of subject, none of these occasions can be dealt with by rule of thumb. Instinct is the king.

Thus Jeannie and I would be there with these three who had the promise of the years before them, each helping us, each so full of secret thoughts and hopes, puzzled, contradictory, timid and brave, obstinate and imaginative. I understood why Jeannie said to me one day that she was grateful for the necessity of cutting lettuces; a humble task, perhaps, but there was more to gain than the price received.

The promise of the years . . . how strange it was, in view of what was to happen, that it should be Shelagh living now in the same caravan a year later, who told us that Julius had died in a motor accident.

Boris in the greenhouse . . .

. . . and outside the front door

11

A year later Geoffrey had left Minack and I had not replaced him.

The high hopes we had once possessed that our extra land and bold plans would materialise into productive success had not become fact. I sold the big tractor, decided to do the heavy work myself and to concentrate mainly on crops in the greenhouses.

Jeannie and I were sad about this apparently backward step. We would, of course, have preferred to have seen our production gathering momentum, but the weather had been consistently against us. In the old days growers used to rely on one good year in four, and that one year compensated them for the three bad ones. Such an attitude is out of the question today. High costs have defeated it.

We were prepared to face this step, however, because we were utterly content in our environment. We never had to wake up in the morning and say to each other that we wished to be somewhere else. We never had to daydream about the perfect home. We were in it.

In London we had known many people who displayed

the outward pageantry of success; the power to demand homage from others, the money and its claim to buy pleasure, the headlines to flatter them, the gush of friends who were not friends, the illusion that to hurry was to go somewhere. We had seen all this, and known its emptiness. Thus, when we surveyed our disappointments, we took courage from our belief that they were trivial compared with the gain.

During April there had been a crisis in Shelagh's life. Her mother by adoption had sold her house in St Buryan and had gone to live in Penzance. In Shelagh's opinion, at that time, Penzance was too far from her work and she set about looking for somewhere else to live. It was a bad time to look. Those who had rooms to let were close to their summer harvest, and they did not relish a permanent guest even if it were Shelagh. By luck, however, we heard that the caravan where Julius had stayed was empty; and the owners, instead of grasping holiday visitors, offered it to Shelagh at a special rent.

How bright was her smile that day she heard the news! She was grown up. She was going to live on her own. She was trusted. And the very next day she brought Jeannie a present, a little cream jug. When she handed it to Jeannie she was blushing, a moment of great shyness, just a quiver of a smile, then a murmur: 'Thank you.'

There were many ways in which Shelagh showed her affection for Jeannie. When she lived in the house at St Buryan she tended the small garden and was very earnest in her efforts. She and Jeannie used to discuss gardens at great length as they worked together, and periodically Shelagh would bring results from her efforts. She brought mint and parsley roots, and one day when Jeannie had expressed a liking for London Pride, Shelagh brought her some the following morning. Another time Jeannie was complaining of the way the west wind roared through a gap into the tiny front garden, and Shelagh replied she knew just the answer. She dug up a veronica bush from her own garden and planted it herself in the offending space. There was another occasion which was specially endearing. She had read in a magazine article how to make a miniature garden. She took great trouble to give it the semblance of Minack and one morning arrived with it in a box, waited until lunchtime and then presented it to Jeannie. It was tragic. The journey from St Buryan had knocked it to pieces and instead of a miniature garden, it was a jumble of tiny debris.

Shelagh had been brought up to be particularly house-proud and there was endless chatter between her and Jeannie on household matters; whether this detergent was better than the other, whether a new furniture polish was as good as it claimed to be; and endless discussions as to the best way to get a shiny black top to the stove. There was also much talk about recipes. Shelagh was constantly producing new ones from magazines and Jeannie would try them out while Shelagh would taste the result. Once, several months before her birthday, she had shown Jeannie a particularly luscious cake recipe and Jeannie, thinking ahead, said to herself that she would do nothing about it until the birthday was due. She told Jane of her plan, baked the cake, and Jane's mother iced it expertly in two shades of blue. Then they gave it to her. For Shelagh it was a moment of sheer enchantment.

She had been trained to perform any house-decorating task with the efficiency of a professional. When Jeannie mentioned she thought it time the walls were painted and the ceiling papered, Shelagh quickly said she would do it. She had the gift, too, of being able to share Jeannie's enthusiasm and they discussed together the colour of the paint and the pattern of the paper as if she, too, were living in the cottage.

Thus her arrival in the caravan did not only provide the delicious sense of the first freedom from continuous contact with older people, but also the chance to put her house-proud instinct and training into practical effect.

The caravan, fifteen minutes on a bicycle from Minack, was a cream utility one. It had long ago lost its wheels and it was raised above the ground by big blocks at its corners. There was an airy space underneath. When I saw this I thought that a westerly gale could pick the caravan up and blow it away with Shelagh inside. I said so.

'Just think of the excitement,' grinned Shelagh. As usual she was enjoying the prospect of drama.

I decided, however, to do something about it, so I got two wire ropes and threw them over the caravan roof, then lashed them to stakes I drove into the ground. Even so, when the westerlies blew, the caravan rocked. It amused Shelagh.

'How did you get on last night?' I would ask, in view of a particularly vicious gale.

'Not bad. Might have been in a dinghy out at sea.'

The caravan did, however, have some special advantages. It had, for instance, a few yards away, a small outhouse in which there was running water, a washbasin and separate lavatory. These were advantages which did not belong to many farm cottages.

Then there was the site. One might not expect many girls to be thrilled about a caravan which was a mile away from a tarmac road; it was more suitable, perhaps, for an eccentric romantic. For the caravan was poised on a small plateau of a field which fell steeply to a wood and a sparkling stream; and this wood and stream shared a companionship until they fell together into the sea. You could see the spot where this happened when you sat in the caravan, down below you perhaps four hundred yards, at the beginning of the sweep of the wild bay with big boulders lining the shore. No sand. It had the tradition of being a beckoning bay which meant that without apparent reason it lured ships to their doom.

Such a notion delighted Shelagh. It appealed to her Grand Guignol romancing. It added spice to her excitement of living alone in such a place; and she ghoulishly suggested that she would play her own part in attracting the doomed ships. She laughingly described how, when the storms were raging, she would dangle a lamp outside her caravan in the tradition of Cornish wreckers.

Within a week of her arrival the utility aura of the caravan had been turned into the cosy atmosphere of a home. Jeannie gave her the blue gingham curtains, and Shelagh made covers for the settee and chair to match. She chose a pink, flower-patterned curtain to separate the little kitchen, where she had a Calor gas stove, from the bedroom. And on the dining table, as one would expect of Shelagh, there would be a bowl of flowers standing on a gaily coloured mat. All the time she was there she kept fresh flowers in that bowl, and if there were none to take back from Minack, she collected wild flowers from the wood in the valley.

The caravan was wired off from the rest of the field so that it was enclosed, together with the outhouse, in a sizeable compound. She promptly cleared up the debris which was lying around and set about turning a section into a kitchen garden. Shelagh was always practical. Behind the shyness, she was a determined person; she now had to buy her own food so she was sensibly taking the opportunity to save money on vegetables.

But this good sense was soon to be countered by an impulsive act which seemed to me to be endearing though foolish. I believed that as she had taken on the responsibility of running her own home for the first time, she ought to settle down and appreciate the problems involved. My attitude, of course, was patronising. It had nothing to do with me how she led her life, and I was reacting perhaps in the same way that a puzzled father is confused by the antics of a teenage daughter. He is near enough in mind to think he understands, but far enough in years to be ignorant.

On a Monday morning, a week after she had become a tenant, she announced to us that on the previous

Saturday afternoon she had bought a mongrel puppy and two kittens from a pet shop.

She was so animated and joyous when she told us the news that I afterwards regretted that I was so cool. My intellect answered her. No emotion. A polite reaction, as if she had told me that she had bought geraniums to decorate her garden. And yet what she had done was what I admired, no sense in it, no logic, not waiting to listen to advice which would have deadened the excitement. She had seen a puppy and two kittens in a window, and she had money in her pocket to buy them and somewhere of her own to give them a home. What she had done possessed the irrational enthusiasm which I had always felt, whatever a person's age, was the beat of life. Here was an act for me to admire, and yet I was frigid.

Jeannie did not react to her in the same way. Jeannie saw quickly that Shelagh was gathering in her arms the lost ones who, like herself, had no permanent home. She could not bear to see their faces looking at her through the shop window. For the first time in her life she had the power to help, and she was not going to make the mistake of letting the moment slip by. Jeannie, because of the nature of her character, was emotionally involved. She agreed with Shelagh on the grounds that a puppy and two kittens had been rescued. Three more animals who had a home. My own coolness was due to my doubt as to what kind of a home Shelagh would give them.

I knew, of course, that Shelagh would give them her love, but how could she look after them when she was away from the caravan every day? Shelagh, even if she had felt emotionally empty, always had lived in a home where the details of her life had been cared for. She never had to bother about the tedious routine which makes the day go round. She did not have to make unwelcome decisions, or make up her mind whether or not to make a self-sacrifice. She was ordered to do something, may have resented it, but she never had to make the mental effort to give the order. She was still a child, and until now she had enjoyed the child's privilege of rebellion without responsibility. Two cats and a dog would certainly test her sense of responsibility.

But I realise now that my doubts were caused by my own personal attitude towards animals. I had developed over the years from a person who treated an animal as a four-legged creature that was pleasant to have around, to a person who was foolish in his devotion. I had become spoilt by the fact that where I worked and where I lived were one and the same place, and so there was no daily break in my relationship with the animal. There were no morning goodbyes and evening reunions. I had become immersed in a continuous relationship. And so it was absurd that I should judge Shelagh or anyone else by the same standard. If an animal receives devotion that is enough, and periods of separation should be considered as a normal hazard in its life.

The kittens were black and white, and she called them Sooty and Spotty. The puppy was a sandy-haired mongrel with a fluffy face like a Yorkshire terrier. She called him Bingo.

The kittens, as one might expect from the self-reliance

of their breed, soon settled down. At first, with the floor of the caravan covered by newspapers, Shelagh kept them indoors while she was away; but as they grew older, the knowledge that the caravan was their home and the source of their food being firmly implanted in their minds, she left a window open. They could come and go as they wished, but they always were there to sleep on her bed at night.

Sooty, in particular, was especially fond of her. When she went into Penzance she used to catch the bus at a place called Boskenna Cross, ten minutes' walk away from the caravan along a lane which was edged by tall trees for part of the way and which passed between farm buildings.

Jeannie and I were in the Land Rover one dark evening when the headlights lit up the figure of Shelagh standing by the bus stop and beside her, to our astonishment was Sooty. We drew up and asked her what he was doing there.

'Oh,' she said, undisguisedly pleased that we had discovered Sooty's affection, 'he often comes with me when I go into town.'

'Yes,' I answered, 'but what happens when you get in the bus and leave him on his own?'

Shelagh, in the bright yellow light, smiled triumphantly.

'He waits,' she said, 'until the nine twenty-five drops me back here.'

It was different with Bingo. A dog is not equipped to provide itself with solitary entertainment. A cat can amuse itself for many quiet hours stalking real or imaginary mice. Any rustle is a challenge. But a dog likes to share its enjoyments. It is extrovert. If a particular pleasure comes its way it wants to tell the whole world how happy it is. A cat is secretive. A dog is generous. A cat can look after itself. A dog is dependent.

The caravan, isolated as it was, still was within barking distance of other isolated homes. Bingo, as it happens, proved to be a remarkably silent dog; but there were times when the cliffs echoed with his noise. Poor Bingo, he was bored. He did not know of the pleasure of hunting imaginary mice.

Shelagh had arranged an elaborate paraphernalia for his happiness. It had been prompted, as most of Shelagh's ideas, by a magazine article. What do you do with a dog, she had read, if you have to be out all day yet possess a small patch where it could be free?

The answer was a long wire fixed at the dog's height between two points, and the dog was attached to this wire from its collar by a hook. Thus, when left on its own, it had the freedom to run up and down; and in Bingo's case he could either stay in the outhouse where he had his basket, food and water, or have a good run outside in the compound.

It was not long, however, before I was saying to myself that we ought to let her bring Bingo to Minack. It was an awkward decision to make, because on our flower farm unless a dog is well controlled it can do a great deal of damage. We had already experienced a dog rushing through daffodil beds in bloom, and another who thought that young tomato plants in the greenhouse were ideal for rolling on.

And yet, of course, we had known some very well-mannered dogs. My cousin, for instance, who lived near St Just, had a beautiful show champion Alsatian named Tara who used to tour the flower farm with the care of a dowager inspecting her garden.

There was another doubt about Bingo. How would he behave towards Boris and Lama? Minack was an oasis where they could wander without danger. It would be unfair to them if they were frightened by a dog. We decided, however, to give Bingo a chance, and so one evening I told Shelagh she could bring him the following day.

She arrived on her bicycle with Bingo on a long lead running beside her. He was an ebullient little dog, and as soon as he saw Jeannie and me he made a dash sideways towards us, nearly pulling Shelagh off the bicycle. And when I saw him do this, a smile on his face as if he were telling me how happy he was to be allowed to stay at Minack, I found myself thinking how pleasant it would be if indeed Shelagh was able to bring him every day. There was the most appealing unity between the two. It is always, of course, to be seen when the years have let flourish a companionship between a man or woman and a dog or a cat; it is to be expected. But there was something special about the look Shelagh gave Bingo as she got off her bicycle. She was pleased with him because he had made a fuss of us; and she was silently telling him so.

Lama was asleep at that particular moment on the bed in the spare room so there was no prospect of trouble as far as she was concerned. The only one we had to worry about was Boris, and yet so endearingly happy was Bingo, rushing about and following Shelagh as she started her work, that I forgot about him. Boris was so independent, so lordly, that I felt sure he could look after himself. And anyhow I was watching Shelagh's face.

I wonder why it was that I was thinking she had a face that would never grow old? As I watched her I knew she was earnestly hoping Bingo would behave with absolute decorum. The picture of a mother who wanted, beyond price of desire, for her child to shine. Every move was judged by the hope of acclamation. Every thought was wishing that Bingo would behave in such a way that he would be accepted.

It is so easy, later, to say that you saw a look in somebody's eye that did not belong to those who will live. Yet, that day Shelagh brought Bingo I sensed that look. There was a fleeting compassion that gave me a chill; for Shelagh yielded the impression that she was trying to put a cloak round Bingo. She wanted him to be loved by someone other than herself. She wanted desperately for us to say that he was a dog we loved, and would look after. All her hopes were dependent on how he behaved on this first day at Minack.

After breakfast I went up to the well to turn on the pump. The engine was in an obstinate mood. I had to take out the plug and clean it, then, as this did not help, adjust the carburettor. I once again vigorously turned the starting-handle and this time the engine fired. Water came spurting out of the thirty-foot pipe and into the tank, and I returned to the cottage with a sense of satisfaction that the water supply was now assured for twenty-four hours. And then, as I came down the path, I heard the most frightful cacophony going on below the cottage.

I ran round the side past the tractor shelter and the greenhouse, and down in front of the flower-house. This was the route that Boris took to and fro from the chicken house; and as I ran I already knew what had happened. Bingo had attacked Boris.

As I arrived Shelagh was taking Bingo, barking hysterically, away, and he looked to me to be so mad with frustration that Shelagh herself was in danger of being bitten. Jeannie, meanwhile, had her hands on Boris who was lying, white wings spread out, on the ground. He was quite still.

'Did you see it happen, Jeannie?'

She had been grading and weighing tomatoes, when she heard the commotion and rushed out to find Bingo pinning Boris to the ground. It was Jeannie, in fact, who first pulled him away, and then Shelagh, realising what had happened, raced from her work to help. When she passed me, she was taking him to the flower-house I had just passed. She was crying.

'Is Boris badly hurt?' I asked Jeannie this question hopefully, because he looked dead to me. He was limp. He was lying with a lifeless abandon. I had seen the same look when, in my youth, I had shot ducks as they came innocently over the Norfolk Broads at dusk.

But as I asked this question Boris began to move, then to struggle free of Jeannie's gentle hands, and to start padding away from us. One wing trailed the ground beside him.

'Thank God,' I said, 'all he's got is a broken wing.'

Here again I was being over-pessimistic. There was no wing broken. Boris had only been behaving in the tradition of wild creatures in a moment of danger. He had been pretending; and as soon as he was a few yards from us, he started to waddle, wings tight to his body, as he had always done. The sudden change in his behaviour made us both laugh. And then I realised that Shelagh had not returned.

'I expect she's soothing Bingo,' Jeannie said.

I now did a stupid thing. I heard Bingo whimpering in the flower-house and I imagined that Shelagh was with him. She had, in fact, gone into the cottage to fetch a jug of warm water and bandages for Boris; but, believing she was with Bingo and wanting to tell her not to be upset, I opened the top half of the stable-type door of the flower-house.

In a second, Bingo, whining like a hyena, was over the top of the lower half of the door, and racing towards Boris again. He was on Boris's back and savaging his neck before Jeannie, very bravely, took him by the scruff of the neck and threw him away; and at that moment Shelagh rushed up, as he was about to take another flying leap at Boris, and picked him up, hugging him to her.

What does one do in such circumstances? Here it was, well before lunchtime and Bingo had already twice attacked Boris; and Lama might too have been a victim if she had not been out of the way in the cottage, and sleeping.

But there was Shelagh. Both Jeannie and I knew what was passing through her mind. Something which she wanted beyond ordinary understanding had failed totally to materialise. She had willed so hard for it to succeed. It was a cornerstone of the new life she was building on her own that those she loved, loved each other. And here, so soon, she was faced with failure. She realised we could not possibly live a life at Minack in which, at any moment, Bingo was poised for the attack. She could not possibly bring him again. And yet, Jeannie and I thought, perhaps if we gave him another chance, for instance, of becoming acclimatised to other beings, he would accept them.

So we compromised by suggesting that she should bring him every day for a week, keeping him on a lead. She could tie him up to a post nearby when she was working in the fields, and if she were indoors or in one of the greenhouses she could leave him in the hut we called the potato-house. It would mean he could get used to us all, and have the comfort of knowing his mistress was with him.

It was no use. Bingo was only quiet when Shelagh was actually beside him. If he saw her from the post to which he was tied or knew she was near when he was shut in the potato-house, the wail of a banshee echoed round Minack.

We had to tell her that she could not bring him.

It was fortunate that shortly afterwards A. P. Herbert came to stay with us. It was particularly fortunate as far as Shelagh was concerned because A.P.H. was co-operating with Russ Conway, who was writing the music, on a version of *A Christmas Carol*. The looks, character, and personality of Russ Conway provided

Shelagh with an ideal. He could do no wrong. He provided her with all the sweetness of first love without the heartbreaks of reality. A photograph, scissored from a magazine, was in her caravan. The only picture of a star she had. And now here was someone actually staying with us who was in regular contact with him.

We did not tell Shelagh what we planned. And when the envelope arrived addressed to her in which, we knew, was a personal letter from Russ Conway and a signed photograph, we handed it to her as casually as if it were a circular.

Half an hour later I called into the flower-house where she was having her lunch. She was sitting with Lama on her lap, the photograph propped against a jam jar beside her, a sandwich in one hand, the letter in the other.

I did not have to ask her whether she was pleased. Nor did she have to say anything. She had the smile of the happiest girl in the world.

Shelagh and Bingo outside her caravan

12

Alan Herbert, during his stay, played an absurd game with Jane and Shelagh when they arrived in the morning. He pretended to take it seriously, and they did too. The game as to check their punctuality not by the normal means of a watch, but by two sundials which he had painstakingly and accurately created.

He called them the Minack Sundials; and one was made from a cocktail tray, the other from the top of a small white table the legs of which he had sawn off.

They had, of course, technical names. The cocktail tray was a Horizontal Sundial, and was allocated to Shelagh because its site was on the arm of the white garden seat which she passed when she arrived in the morning. The table top was an Equatorial Sundial, and so placed that Jane came face to face with it as soon as she jumped over the hedge from her hurried journey across the fields.

I have no idea how A.P.H. made his calculations, but they continued over a period of days and whatever was happening, wherever we might be, we always had to hurry back to the sundials at one o'clock. The purpose was to compare the shadow on the dial he had drawn with the pips of the Greenwich time signal. When at last he was satisfied that accuracy had been assured, he issued the Minack Sundial Instructions; a copy for Jane, a copy for Shelagh.

Unfortunately as his handwriting is very difficult to decipher without the help of a magnifying glass, the girls looked at the instructions in wonderment but without comprehension.

'The Cocktail Tray Sundial,' Shelagh could have read, 'should be dead level, but is warped already.'

'The Table Top Sundial,' Jane may have seen, 'has hour spaces which should be exactly equal . . . but one or two, I fear, are not.'

Jane was also informed in these instructions, 'the dial, believe it or not, is parallel with the Equator which will, I am sure, be a great source of satisfaction.'

Neat diagrams accompanied the instructions and there was an extra page on which was listed the Equation of Time. This was to prove confusing in judging the girls' punctuality because, as sundial owners will know, dials do not coincide with the clock. In August the dial can be as much as six minutes ahead, and in September nine minutes behind. So when the girls arrived for work it was not just a question of looking at the dial. There had to be a mathematical calculation as well.

However, this did not deter A.P.H. He was up every morning at a quarter to eight, waiting. It was a ritual he would not miss, and he was only thwarted when a cloud hid the sun.

'Get away you cloud!' he would shout to the heavens.

And if it did, the sun shining once again on his cocktail tray and his table top, he would greet with mock solemnity first Shelagh: 'You're early by two minutes' . . . and then Jane: 'Jane! By your Equatorial Sundial you are three and a half minutes late.'

One morning A.P.H. was still waiting for Jane three-quarters of an hour after she was due to arrive. He was standing by the Equatorial Sundial calling out the minutes: 'Forty-four, forty-five . . .' when she came panting apologetically over the hedge to say that Lamb had disappeared. Lamb, the sheep, which Jane and her mother had taken pity on when it was a few weeks old.

'She was on the grass outside the cottage when we went to bed last night,' she said, 'but there is no sign of her anywhere this morning.'

Lamb led an unusual life for a sheep. She was favoured as if she were a dog. She could come in and out of the cottage as she wished, and when she was in the mood she would join Eva and Acid the dogs, Polly the parrot, Sim and Val the cats, for a share of the food at mealtimes. She was part of the household. And at night she either slept in the garden, in a small hut when the weather was bad, or in the grass field on the other side of the garden wall.

'Perhaps someone has stolen her for her fleece,' I said. She had a fine fleece which was about ready to be sheared. 'Anyhow, Jane,' I added, 'you go straight back to get on with your search, and we'll follow you.'

It was a strange coincidence that Lamb should have chosen this moment to disappear. She had been looked after and loved by Jane's family for over five years. They were her life. I used to pass by their cottage and see her lying in the doorway, reminding me of a Newfoundland dog. She would never be able to get used to other people. Nobody would treat her in the same kind way that Jane and her mother and Jeremy had done. It was a coincidence because, only a few days before, Jane had broken the news to us that they had to give up the cottage. The farm had been sold. Her mother was leaving to take a job on Tresco in the Isles of Scilly; and on Tresco island no dogs were allowed or, one might expect, a pet sheep. Thus a new home would have to be found for Lamb.

'And what are you yourself going to do, Jane?' I had asked.

'Oh, I'm going to stay here. I'll find somewhere to live.'

I loved her assurance. I realised that sooner or later she would go to join her mother but she would not leave us suddenly. She was loyal to Jeannie and me. She had that blessed quality which enhanced the stature of those with whom she associated. Jeannie and I felt the better when she was with us. She had the gift of infecting us with her enthusiasm, and she exuded a sense of honesty.

'You can come and stay with me,' Shelagh said, who was in the flower-house at the time, 'there's the outhouse to store your things in, and there's plenty of room in the caravan for you.'

'But there'll be the dogs,' said Jane.

'Oh, Bingo won't mind.'

I took no part in this conversation. It was nothing to do with me. But I wondered what on earth would happen if Bingo, Eva, Acid, and now Acid's pup, should all be left together for the day long.

We searched the cliffs all morning for Lamb, and clambered down on to the rocks in case she had fallen over. We called at neighbouring farms in case she had wandered to them. Nobody had seen her. And we were beginning to think that she might indeed have been stolen, when Jane suddenly discovered her. She had meandered away from the cottage, down a steep path to the wooded valley where a stream rushes to the sea. When she reached the stream she must have slipped and fallen over. For she was lying in the rushes upside down. She was dead.

This incident developed my feeling of impending sadness. I was influenced, no doubt, by its reminder that a period was ending, the usual sentimental sense of loss which pervades the finish of a chapter of one's life.

It seemed the wink of an eyelid since we first saw Jeremy playing with Acid outside their cottage on the grass, throwing a ball at her, Acid retrieving it, on and on, hour after hour. Or the first time we saw Jeremy with a fishing rod taller than himself, and holding a tiny rock fish in his hand. 'A very menacing-looking fish, don't you think?' he had suggested. Or when we first met Jane's mother, tall and young-looking, coming up the path from the little well they used, and telling us that if we employed Jane we would find her 'very pain-staking'. Or that day Jane first came to Minack; and the way she was determined to get the job. Their cottage had seemed without character when we first saw it; but now it would always be alive. We would never be able to pass it without remembering the happiness of the Wyllie family.

At the end of September I loaded the back of the Land Rover with Jane's belongings and drove them over to Shelagh's caravan. A carrier had already taken an advance load which included Jane's harmonium; and when I arrived I found it almost completely filled Shelagh's outhouse. Jane was determined to keep it at all costs. And indeed, when in due course she left to join her mother on Tresco, the harmonium went too; the last part of its journey being in a motor boat from the main island of St Mary's. By this time Acid and her pup had been sent to Jane's married sister; and an exception was made for Eva on Tresco because of her old age and minute size.

Jane's attitude to a car she and her mother had bought had to be different. It was a little saloon car which they had proudly bought second-hand. It was, however, an unfortunate bargain for they seldom were able to persuade the engine to start. It remained immovable in the backyard of the cottage for month after month, and its only virtue was to provide sleeping quarters for the cats. After her mother left, Jane set out to sell it; and the best offer she received was five pounds for the tyres.

I remember Jane's fury. It was an insult; and although she was now living in Shelagh's caravan, her mother in the Scillies, the cottage belonging to a stranger, she indignantly turned down the offer. The car was left where it always had been. A year later it was still there.

She stayed with Shelagh for a month, and then had the luck to be offered a small cottage close by that was let to holiday visitors in the summer. It was still not certain when she would join her mother, and so the routine at Minack went on as usual. She would arrive with Shelagh, both on their bicycles, in the morning, and because it was November and the gales were often blowing and rain whipped the land, Jeannie or I would drive them home in the evening, bicycles in the back of the Land Rover. It was part of the charm of their natures that, the journey ended, they thanked us always so freshly.

The routine revolved mostly around work in the greenhouses where we were growing freesias, spray chrysanthemums, and forget-me-nots; while outside we had wallflowers, anemones and a few stocks and violets. We were no longer growing on a massive scale in the open. We had daffodils, of course, but these would not be beginning to bloom until the end of January.

Jeannie and I were, in fact, conducting a rearguard action. We had been bruised in recent seasons. We had lost a little of our confidence. We were no longer ebullient optimists. We were aiming to play safe; and the cornerstone of the safety had been Jane and Shelagh. They knew our ways, and spurred us on when we were doubtful.

I do not believe age determines whether or not you can be on the same wavelength as another. There is simply a meeting of minds of whatever age which instantly feel at ease, just as there are other times when people, hard as they may try to prevent it, find they resent each other, or are bored. Thus a child can find that his thoughts are fluent, so, too, the means to express them with one teacher, while an hour later, in another class, he finds himself dumb. All he has done has been to be with one teacher who was on his wavelength, another who was not.

There was the incident of the chrysanthemums when, as I was the boss and the mistake was entirely my fault, both Jane and Shelagh could, perhaps, have been justified in reacting with lofty superiority.

There was frost at the beginning of December and it was my job to light the paraffin heaters in the greenhouses. The one in the chrysanthemum house was an elaborate affair, and one night when I lit it, I forgot to replace an important section of the apparatus. It was the vital section which turned the paraffin from smoke into heat. Thus when next morning I arrived at the greenhouse the chrysanthemums resembled the uninhibited dream of a chimney sweep. The leaves and buds of our precious flowers were covered with soot. I felt very ashamed.

'There's been an accident,' I said, after the girls had come swishing over the gravel on their bicycles in the morning, 'and' I added, as if I were relieved at the confession, 'it is entirely my fault . . . believe it or not!'

They, of course, made their comments. I was prepared for that. I knew I was destined for a day of being chided, but then I deserved it.

'Don't you think, Mrs Tangye, that we ought to give him a chimney sweep's outfit for Christmas?'

'Soap powder and scrubbing brush would be better!' said Shelagh.

The four of us spent half the morning blowing and

puffing the soot off the plants. It was hard work, and if a stranger had seen us I am sure he would have thought we had gone mad. We looked like four people blowing out an endless supply of candles; and we were so slow that I began to wonder whether we could complete the job in the day. Then Shelagh had a bright idea.

'Why don't we use our bicycle pumps?'

'Shelagh,' I said, 'you're a genius. Of course, that's the answer!'

And it was. Thanks to the bicycle pumps the chrysanthemums in due course were successfully disposed of in Covent Garden.

It is strange, in retrospect, that none of us ever had a warning about Shelagh. Neither Jane nor Jeannie nor I, nor Pat, the girl she saw most evenings and every weekend, none of us can look back and remember some incident that might have given us a clue. She loved her long bicycle rides with Pat, never showing any signs of tiredness; and never once at Minack did Jeannie or I have to say: 'Shelagh doesn't look very well today.' She never complained. She was never lethargic. And I do not believe she missed one day's work in all the time she was with us.

And yet I wonder sometimes whether I had an intuition there was danger ahead, and which I did not recognise except in my subconscious. Jeannie, too, feels that she had this intuition. Certainly the two of us acted in a strangely protective way towards her, a way that was not inspired by any awareness that something might be wrong.

I, for instance, found myself steering her away from work which tested her strength. She had, of course, baskets of flowers to carry, but I found myself always turning to Jane when I was needing help with my manual labour. My choice was not deliberately made. I just knew instinctively that Jane was the stronger.

Thus it was Jane who used to accompany me as I struggled with trimming hedges and cutting the grass of the daffodil meadows. I had two instruments which I used, a hedge cutter and a motor scythe; and both of them, while leaving me exhausted after an hour or two of using them, also required considerable stamina on the part of my helper. I also required Jane's patience and humour; for both hedge cutter and scythe were my enemies.

The hedge cutter, as long as a fishing rod and as heavy as a sack of potatoes, was fastened to me by a strap across my shoulders; and I used to advance along the chosen hedge, my hands clasping the handles of the hedge cutter, my arms bringing the fast-moving blade in a downward sweep, while Jane with a fork speedily swept the cuttings away. It was her speed which eased my labour. If my downward sweep was checked so that the blade was blocked by the debris it had cut, there would be a splutter and the engine would stop.

I would then swear. Jane, on the other hand, because she had grown accustomed to the inevitability that the engine would sometimes stop, appeared not to listen but continued to collect the cuttings into heaps. She also knew that a period of swearing was scheduled because the hedge cutter's engine would almost certainly prove difficult to restart.

The performance was repeated with the motor scythe. I would lunge with a thin cord to get it started, and then career through a meadow, cutting a path while Jane pulled the grass quickly to one side. If she was not quick enough, the motor scythe would also get blocked and the engine stall; and my swearing would begin as before.

It is odd, but engines seldom have operated at Minack in a normal fashion. Engineers called to make them go again have repeatedly remarked that the engine fault has never been known before. One firm lightheartedly suggested they should put up a tent so that their engineer could regularly be on the premises to mend one particular rotovator. On another occasion, after a brand new rotovator, specially delivered, remained obstinately silent, the sales manager made the journey from the Midlands to see what was wrong. And as usual his comment was: 'Never known it before.'

Jane maintained that the pixies were at work. They resent the noise, she alleged, and so at night silenced the engines. It was all wrong, and futile, that mechanisation should reign on these ancient cliffs; the ghosts were angry, for their values were being challenged; the values which had stood for a horizon of time. Challenged by instruments impervious to loyalty.

There was one tractor, the big one which we sold, that excelled in obstinacy while at Minack; yet as soon as it was taken away and put to work somewhere else, it behaved with perfection. While we had it, for instance, the hydraulic system which lifted the plough would only operate when it was in the mood; and this was seldom.

Thus we were always asking for mechanics, and the mechanics were always saying, after two or three hours' hard work, that they had never known the fault before. I used to become distraught.

'Jeannie,' I would cry, after a mechanic's visit, 'you won't believe what he said . . .' Jeannie did not have to pause; 'I know, I know. . .'

When the day came that I sold this particularly large tractor, the purchaser explained that he would send a lorry to collect it on the following day. I told Jane.

'Well,' she said, rubbing her hands together and answering me as if she were a conspirator, 'what about getting up very early and ploughing that piece above the greenhouse we want?'

Her idea was an excellent one. It was a piece of ground bordered by ditches which had been dug by me because of the clinging wetness of the land. If I ploughed it myself I would not only save the expense of a contractor, but I would also speed the opportunity to begin using the land.

The lorry was expected at ten in the morning, so I got up at six; and by eight, when Jane arrived, I had almost completed the job. There is a clean, powerful sense of ambition achieved if you are ploughing a piece of land; and it is a beautiful morning, woodpeckers laughing, blackbirds singing, indeed all the birds you live with throughout the year, are exulting in a blue sky and a warm sun. Gulls were following my furrow, so too jackdaws that came from Pentewan cliffs opposite Jane's cottage, and robins and chaffinches. As I went up and down the field I rejoiced I had sold the tractor. It was no longer a hulk of metal to worry about. By the evening I would have forgotten its existence.

And then, on this lovely morning with Jane now walking up and down behind the plough, turning over the furrows with her foot, the furrows which the plough itself had failed to turn over, I backed the tractor, and a wheel fell into one of my ditches.

'Jane!' I cried out in anguish, 'I'm stuck. I can't get out!'

It was the front right-hand wheel, a small wheel compared with one of the rear wheels; and it was lodged two feet in the ditch, tilting the tractor so that it looked from where Jane was standing as though it might turn over.

She was laughing at me, fair hair against rich brown earth, eight in the morning and a pagan rejoicing in a joke that might have been of her own making. The tractor stuck, me in a panic, the purchaser on his way with a lorry.

'All right, all right, all right,' I said, 'it's all jolly funny, but what are we going to do about it?'

I knew, better than she did, that it might be a major performance to get that wheel out of the ditch.

'I'll push.'

She pushed while I revved the engine, but the rear wheels, which the engine powered, revolved without any wish to grip the earth.

'Push harder.'

Jane, in rubber boots for a change, was shoving at the tractor, a shoulder pressed to the mudguard, as if she were a female Hercules.

223

'Give it a little bit more,' and as I said this my foot was on the accelerator, the engine was roaring, and the time was nearing nine o'clock, 'you look as if you can move a mountain . . . so do it!'

And she did.

The tractor suddenly gave a lurch, the wheel cleared the ditch, and I was out on the level ground again.

'Jane, dear,' I said, 'well done!'

'Yes, sir,' she replied with mannered and humorous politeness, 'but, if I may say so, you don't put a tractor in the ditch two hours before the purchaser collects it!'

Jeannie's intuition about Shelagh concerned her bicycle journeys. She was always saying to her that she should not embark on these marathon rides. And Shelagh just smiled and did not take any notice.

'Oh, I'm all right,' Shelagh would say, 'you don't have to worry about me.'

But Jeannie still worried, and as the winter grew fiercer, she continued to drive Shelagh home. Then in January it became obvious that life in a caravan on a Cornish hillside with gales rocking the caravan every night, torrential storms damping the inside, was scarcely suitable for a girl by herself who was not yet twenty. And so Shelagh decided to move into Penzance and live with her mother by adoption.

Again Jeannie experienced an intuitive sense of apprehension.

'Now, Shelagh,' she said, though of course it was not her duty to impose her views, 'mind you use the bus and not your bicycle. It's too far by bike.'

Shelagh smiled at her. The delicious smile we knew so well.

'I'll see,' she said. And then, reminding us of what we already knew, 'I always biked to and from St Buryan when I was working in Penzance.'

For a while she did as Jeannie had asked her, and at the day's end we would drive her up the long lane to the bus stop. It was a sensible arrangement, and we were glad that she had agreed with us.

But one morning she arrived again by bicycle, and the next and the next. Spring was in the air, she explained, and she loved to feel the soft air in her face.

She never came by bus again.

13

When the three of them, Shelagh, Jane and Jeannie, were in the flower-house bunching, Boris would waddle at intervals to the open door.

He would stick out his long white neck, waggle his tail feathers, and peer at them with a beady eye.

'Here you are, Boris.'

And one of them would throw him a broken biscuit.

There was always a supply of broken biscuits, cake and breadcrumbs on the flower-bench table. Jane and Shelagh made it their business to see that this larder was kept full, because it was not only Boris who expected to be fed. There was a constant coming and going of chaffinches, robins, bluetits and tomtits, a whirring of wings as the flowers were bunched.

There were, of course, favourites among them. Shelagh favoured the lady chaffinch that seemed to be Charlie's wife, and Jeannie preferred Charlie, who was now just as noisy as the first Charlie, and we all loved Tim, the robin.

'Where's Tim?'

'He's in deep thought ... up there on that jar of anemones.'

He would perch for an hour on end, quite still, looking down on the work in progress. Then suddenly he would treat us to a warble. A whispered warble. A warble so muted that we had to smile.

'A little louder, please,' would come Jane's own quiet little voice. But Tim would continue to warble as softly as before.

He especially enjoyed standing on one leg on a thick black-painted beam which stretched across the flower-house; and it was here that I last saw him. It was a beam on which we used to staple the prize cards we had won at the Penzance Flower Shows; and this gave us an opportunity to make idle jokes about him.

'Tim's in a first prize mood today' ... because he was perched directly above that card. Or at another time: 'Tim feels only like a third prize this morning.'

We never knew what happened. He just disappeared. For a few days we were unperturbed by his absence because there had been previous times when he had gone off; and then returned. On one occasion he even vanished for a month or two, and then to my joy I found him once again in the flower-house. This time four, six, eight, ten weeks passed by, and there was no sign of him. We were still hoping for his return when, just before Christmas, Jane at last left to join her mother in the Scilly Isles. Tim never came back, but Jane did.

She came back for the Penzance Flower Show.

This show, the Western Commercial Horticultural

Spring Show to give it its full title, is the first mainland flower show of the year, and it takes place on two days in the first week or two of March. It is a beautiful show, for here you see daffodils and so many other kinds of flowers which provide the true herald of spring. They are not unnatural, forced flowers. They are flowers from the Cornish cliffs and the Scilly Isles. Flowers that last longer in the home, because they are not sickened by man-made efforts to bring them into bloom before their time.

As the date of each Show approached there used to be much excitement at Minack. We would be in the middle of the flower harvest, a hectic period of rush in which there was paramount necessity to send away to market as many flowers as possible, as quickly as possible. I was consumed by my urge to do this; and as a result I was placed in mild conflict with Jeannie, Jane and Shelagh. True enough they pursued their work as diligently as ever, but there was a hint in their manner that suggested that their minds were on the following week.

Their talk in the flower-house would dwell on our entries in the various classes. Instead of concentrating their attention on picking and bunching as quickly as possible, I would realise they were keeping a constant look-out for prospective prize-winning blooms. I would find, for instance, superb wallflowers or forget-me-nots or violets hidden away in jam jars in dark corners.

'Jeannie,' I would exclaim in exasperation, 'we simply cannot afford to go into the Show this year. You must tell the girls to forget about it. They must be made to realise their wages depend on the speed we get our flowers away.'

No notice was taken of me. Every year I reacted in the same way. Every year I relented. Every year I was as delighted as the rest to see our entries displayed. Thus they tolerated my initial poor humour.

'Don't take any notice of him,' said Jeannie good-naturedly, after I had raged over a glorious collection of freesias I had found in the dark of the stables. Jane had thought I would never find them.

Both Jane and Shelagh adored this pre-excitement to the Show. It added spice to their day. My attitude made them feel conspirators; and I, looking from the outside, aware that I was displaying tantrums which were not really tantrums, was touched by the intangible love and understanding between them and Jeannie. They all mocked me.

Up there on the beam were the prize cards Minack flowers had won. First for wallflowers, first in successive years for freesias, first for lettuces; and there were the firsts for one of the gems of the Show, the packed box of mixed commercial flowers grown by the exhibitor. Jeannie won this two years running, and then it was decided to allow bought flowers to be included in the box. Yet Jeannie, despite the bought flowers, again won first prize and the cup with Minack-grown flowers.

Jane was always an ardent exhibitor, and she did so from the sheer joy she derived from placing on show something as near perfect as she could make it. When she was only sixteen she won the first prize in the Floral Art class.

Her exhibit was a small sandwich tin in which was placed a little nest of dried grass lined with gleanings of Monty's fur. In the nest were three tiny blue Easter eggs which she had bought at Woolworths. Around the nest she had built up a mossy bank in which were primroses, violets, forget-me-nots and behind these, miniature daffodils. It was beautiful.

Now when she came back, a year later, in reply to our invitation to stay at Minack for the Show, she brought with her the entries from the famous Tresco Gardens where she now worked. She was in sole charge of these entries. She had chosen the blooms herself and it was her job to prepare them, then arrange them on the stands. Five years after she first came to Minack, she was competing on her own with the best growers in Cornwall.

Jeannie met her in the Land Rover when the *Scillonian* docked at Penzance. It was a calm day of blue sky and innocence, and when Jane greeted Jeannie she described the trip across as the best she had ever made. So too had been her trip in the launch from Tresco to St Mary's; and thus her boxes, several boxes of various daffodils and flowering shrubs, had received no buffeting. They now awaited Jane's care and discretion as to how they would be presented in Penzance's St John's Hall the following day; for the exhibits, Jeannie's also, of course, had to be staged by the exhibitors by ten o'clock on the Wednesday evening.

Jeannie welcomed Jane as an ally, for as usual my anxiety for material results was clashing with my desire to help the Show by exhibiting.

'He's just the same, Jane.'

Jane smiled.

'Well, we've learned not to listen to him!'

It was, of course, imperative that Jane's flowers should be put in water as quickly as possible; but there was also an added apprehension as far as flower show exhibitors are concerned. Would the blooms be in their full glory at the instant the judges passed by?

Jane had erred, if this is erring, in picking her blooms when they were truly fresh, when the buds were just bursting. Yet if the buds did not come into their perfection within thirty-six hours, her efforts would be ignored.

For the prize she was really aiming for, quite apart from the other entries she had planned, was the top accolade of Cornish and Scilly Isle growers, the Prince of Wales Cup.

Only the most illustrious names of growers had been inscribed as the winners. What were her chances?

'The best thing to do, Jane,' I said, 'is to put them in the big greenhouse. The tomatoes we've planted are being kept at a temperature of fifty degrees, and that will bring out your daffodils at just the right speed. No forcing, just naturally.'

So the daffodils, on the Tuesday afternoon, were put there, carefully placed in pails by Jane. They were called Carbineer. An elegant yellow daffodil with a red cup, an aristocrat among the many others striving for the public's attention.

That evening Jeannie, Jane and I went down to see Tommy and Hilda Bailey at the Lamorna Inn. These two, ever since we first came to Minack, had given us encouragement and advice; and if we had a gardening problem we usually sought Tommy's opinion. He was an expert flower-grower.

'Fifty degrees is the right temperature for Jane's daffs, don't you think, Tommy?'

'Certainly. We always reckoned that temperature in the old days.'

Tommy looked at Jane. He had often come to Minack, and worked with Jane and ourselves. And he sensed her excitement.

'Jane, my love,' he said, 'don't you worry . . . you're going to win.'

When we left Lamorna a wind was rushing up the valley, and as the headlights of the Land Rover stretched along the road, lighting up the swaying trees on either side, I felt concerned.

'A gale's blowing up,' I said, as I turned the corner to Minack, 'it'll play havoc with the California unless it eases by morning.'

I went to bed and slept well, but I was awakened at six o'clock by Lama jumping on to the bed, and miaowing.

'Shut up, Lama,' I murmured, 'you can't go out yet.'

Then suddenly I was savaged from the comfort of my sleepiness by the roar of the wind. It was a sea wind, tearing in across Mount's Bay.

'Wake up, Jeannie! We must get the California in as quickly as possible. I'll go ahead and start picking.'

How often we had raced against a gale to gather our daffodils before they were so bruised and damaged that they were fit only for the compost heap! How often I had bent down between the beds, blown sometimes off my balance, desperately clutching in one hand the stems I had struggled to pick with the other! Yet it was a task which provided much satisfaction once the basket had been carried safely into the flower-house . . . and when the gale continued to roar hour after hour reminding me every minute that a harvest had been saved. This is what was to happen that Wednesday.

I was followed down to the California meadow by Jeannie and then, a few minutes afterwards, by a dozy Jane. I had ruthlessly asked Jeannie to wake her up.

'Sorry about this, Jane,' I shouted into the wind. I was only politely sorry. I was, of course, thankful to see her once again in a Minack meadow.

And when within an hour the meadow was cleared and the daffodils were safe in the flower-house, I said to the two of them that we could now spend the rest of the day in peace. I had not guessed that we were about to experience the most ferocious gale in the Penzance area within living memory.

As soon as breakfast was over, Jeannie and I started to bunch the daffodils we would be sending by the afternoon flower train, while Jane began to sort out her various exhibits. There was a great deal of work for her to do. She was thus content to leave the Carbineer in the greenhouse, for she believed that another hour or two in the warmth would form the blooms to perfection. She needed twenty-four bunches, twelve blooms in each, to be packed in two boxes, as her entry for the

Prince of Wales Cup. Also two perfect bunches to be placed in vases above the boxes.

'I think I'm right, don't you?'

'It can't do any harm, Jane.'

That was at nine o'clock.

At ten I said to Jeannie: 'Am I imagining it or is it in fact blowing twice as hard as when we were picking the California?'

'Frankly,' she said, and she was smiling at me, 'I'm terrified.'

'What about you, Jane?'

'It does sound a bit rough. I think I'll get the Carbineer.'

They were in the big greenhouse in front of the cottage and so, when Jane collected them she had only to dash from the flower-house perhaps twenty yards there and back.

I opened the flower-house door for her. It swung viciously on its hinges so that a gust whipped inside.

'Look out,' called Jeannie, 'those daffs are knocked over!'

The gust had indeed knocked over two jars of daffodils Jeannie was keeping for the Show. But, instead of sympathising with her, I was transfixed by a sight which I had never seen before and hope will never see again.

'Jeannie!' I called out, 'The greenhouse is going!'

The greenhouse was swaying like a tree. A hundred feet long and twenty feet wide, it was lurching first to one side, then to the other; and I suddenly saw a terrible suction effect which made the glass roof appear to leap upwards. A pause; and then the whole massive structure began swaying again. And all the while there was the roar of the gale, so deafening, that although I was standing just outside the flower-house Jeannie could not hear my shouts. I went back inside.

'Jane,' I said, 'I'm sorry. The greenhouse will crash any second. You can't possibly fetch your flowers.'

'It'll only take a minute!'

'Jane,' I repeated firmly, 'you can't do it. If you open the greenhouse door that will be the end.'

There was plenty of work inside the flower-house to keep us busy. Jane had her other exhibits to attend to, while Jeannie and I had to bunch the daffodils that filled the galvanised pails lining the shelves. Bunching can be a peaceful task that allows your thoughts to roam. You bunch automatically. You instinctively select the blooms, three to each row, then two rubber bands to hold the stems, and another bunch is done. A therapeutic task if you are not expecting to hear, at any second, the crash of breaking glass.

'I'm going out to have a look at the mobiles.'

I could not pretend to be calm like Jeannie and Jane appeared to be. My nerves were too raw to cope with routine. I could not confine myself to the flower-house. I felt impelled to watch the destruction which seemed inevitable. I went outside and struggled up the lane to the mobiles; and for ten minutes watched uselessly and with fascination. Then I came back and stared at the big greenhouse. Through the glass I could see Jane's Carbineer in their pails. Never, I thought, had daffodils that were scheduled for the Prince of Wales Cup been in such danger.

At lunchtime Jane said she thought the gale was easing.

'You're an optimist.'

'I think it's easing too,' said Jeannie.

'You're both optimists.'

As the time passed there was, in fact, no pause in its violence. It thundered on and on. The noise was so terrible that sometimes I thought it was the collapse of the greenhouse that I had heard. Then I would look, and miraculously it was still intact.

At three o'clock I loaded the flower boxes destined for Covent Garden into the back of the Land Rover. I was thankful that action was required of me. I would now be doing something that demanded all my concentration and for an hour I would be relieved from watching the heaving, swaying greenhouses. I could balance my own fears by seeing what had happened to others.

I reached Newlyn Bridge and a policeman turned me left into the Coombe. The coast road was impassable. Great gaps had been ground from the sea wall. I joined the line of traffic that travelled up Alverton, through the town and to the station. On the platform the indefatigable George and Barry, who handled the flower cargoes, greeted me with the news that I was just in time. The evening tide, they reckoned, would flood Penzance station and cut the railway line which ran to Marazion parallel to the shore. It did.

When I got back to Minack an hour and a half later, I drove down the lane murmuring to myself that all

I could expect to see was debris; and I found myself wondering what one did with heap upon heap of broken glass. But first I saw the Robinson mobiles were still there. Then the big greenhouse. I marvelled at our good fortune and my reaction as soon as I pulled up at the cottage was to find Jeannie so that I could share my pleasure.

The storm by now was reaching its peak. Seldom does a gale maintain its momentum for hour after hour, viciously hitting the innocent, as if it were a cruel boxer who was meeting no opposition. But as Wednesday afternoon turned into evening, and growers all over the area were desperately arranging their long-planned entries for the Show, the storm increased. By eight o'clock that evening it was diabolical.

I had got back and found Jane bunching her Carbineer.

'Heavens, Jane, how did you get them?'

I knew it was an unnecessary question. Jane and Jeannie were in league together and as soon as I was out of the way they had proceeded to carry out what they had already planned. They watched the canvas hood of the Land Rover disappear. Then they acted. Within a few minutes, Jane had hopped into the greenhouse and brought out her flowers.

Of course, I was delighted she had done it. I had been spared any sense of responsibility, Jeannie's support had been justified, and now we could all hope that Jane would win.

At nine o'clock the Land Rover was ready to go into Penzance again. There were seven entries from Jane and six entries from Jeannie, and they were placed in the well of the Land Rover as if they were jewels. Along with them went enthusiasm, tenacity and courage.

Knocker, successor to Hubert

14

Jane won the Prince of Wales Cup, the youngest competitor ever to do so.

She also won four other first prizes including three more cups. And when we came back to Minack after she had been presented with her trophies, we were given a welcome which belonged to the life Jane had lived with us.

Knocker, the gull, was on the roof; Lama was rolling on the path looking inviting; and Boris waddled towards us and followed us up to the door. The gale was over. They were all at ease again.

As for ourselves, we were bewildered by the strain and the success. We were all very quiet. I remember coming into the cottage and saying to Jane what a wonderful experience it had been for Jeannie and me that the schoolgirl who had once called on us for a job had won such a victory. The sound of the storm was still in my ears. I was still dazed.

Then suddenly I heard Jane's soft voice; and what

she said brought to the surface why, in fact, we were so quiet.

'How Shelagh would have loved these past two days!'

Jane was sitting on the same chair where she sat the day she first came to Minack. Jeannie was sitting opposite her on the sofa. I picked up a pipe from my desk and began to fill it.

'A year ago she was celebrating her prize for bunched violets. She was so pleased with that win,' I said.

The gull was crying up on the roof.

'What happened to Bingo?' Jane asked.

'The RSPCA found a good home for him . . . Spotty and Sooty were put to sleep when she left the caravan. They were ill.'

There was silence for a moment. Then I said: 'She didn't suffer. She was unconscious even when she fell off her bicycle. When she was a child she had been in hospital with heart trouble.'

'She never showed any signs that anything was wrong while I was with her.'

'None of us had any warning.'

Jeannie was stroking Lama who had jumped on her lap.

'You were great friends, Jane,' she said, 'I will always remember you together.'

'Oh yes. She was coming to stay with us on Tresco last Easter, the week she died.'

Jeannie turned to her; and at this instant I found myself seeing again Shelagh's delicious smile when she was very happy.

'Just think, Jane,' Jeannie said, 'how glad she would be for you today.'

*Jane, after winning
first price at
Penzance Flower Show*